lakiriboto chronicles
a brief history of badly behaved women

ayodele olofintuade

For all the women that came before me,
women who raised me, Apinke, Abeke,
Apeke, Asake, Adenike, Olaide, Iyabode,
Morieba, Adebimpe, Adetayo, Olubanke,
Tokunbo.
To innumerable others who have had my
back, Chris, Bibi, Adunni, Lola, Kafayat,
Michelle, Rafeeat, Kehinde, Tolulope,
Adenike, Titilope, Dupe, Abiola,
Charmaine, Azafi.
For all the women who tread in the
footsteps of the ancestors.

© Ayodele Olofintuade, 2018

ISBN: 978-978-921-117-91

all rights reserved
no part of this publication may be reproduced, stored in a retrieval system or transmitted in any form or by any means, electronic, mechanical, photocopying, recording, or otherwise without the expressed written consent of the author, who is the copyright owner.

Published in Nigeria by
Bookbuilders Editions Africa
2, Awosika Avenue, Old Bodija, Ibadan
bookbuilders@yahoomail.com
+234 805 662 9266

Printed in Ibadan by
Jungle Urchins, Publications
jungleurchins@gmail.com
+234 705 965 3854

season 1
a glass half empty (2005)

a death

Moremi discovered Alhaja in a sleep that was as deep as it was infinite, around 6:30am that Saturday morning. The bed-sheet and blanket were tangled together to one side of the bed, it was as if she had engaged Death in a battle, and lost, because nothing Moremi did would wake her up - despite calling her name repeatedly, and shaking her, first gently and then vigorously.
Her heart raced faster than her legs as she dashed out of the house into the courtyard, hoping somebody, anybody, would join in her bid to wake Alhaja up from her death sleep.
In her eleven year old mind, her grandmother could still be rescued, snatched out of the bloodied hands of death before her spirit crossed to the other side, a vague place that could be in the heavens above, underneath the earth or just a spitting distance.
She paused in front of the low fence that separated her home from the other houses in the neighbourhood, and stood on tiptoes. After about two minutes without even the whisper of feet, Moremi ran to the gate and pulled it open, but then she remembered her grandmother's warning about gbómo-gbómo - men and women that prowled their street, turning wandering children into yams, before kidnapping them. .
She shut the gate and stood indecisively, for a moment, then remembered the bungalows located in the backyard.
She followed a tiny path that wound drunkenly between the mango, and bush cherry trees, and drew to a stop when she got to the three small bungalows fighting for space amongst the trees.
Moremi checked each bungalow for signs of life, the doors were locked, the wooden shutters firmly closed. It was as if Alhaja had dragged every living soul with her to the other side.

Alhaja can't be dead, they had still been together the previous night watching the TV, and her grandmother hadn't looked or acted like someone who was planning to die. In fact she and her brother, Olori Ebi, had a good time, taking shots from the bottle of schnapps he'd brought for her.

She pulled the stories of night markets, where the living and dead mingled, that her grandmother had told her over the years around her, a comforting blanket, because nobody ever dies, not truly.

Alhaja is not dead, she chanted, Alhaja is not dead, over and again.

She was so engrossed in her thoughts, that when she stepped out of the last bungalow she tripped over the root of one of the trees, and fell flat on her face. Moremi tried not to cry as she pulled herself off the ground, she knew once she started she wouldn't be able to stop.

She took several deep breaths, held on to a tree trunk, and pulled herself up. She checked for bruises, there was a large one on her left shin, *Alhaja will take care of it once she wakes up*, she reassured herself, and called out again.

"Mama Seun! Mama Adija!"

Neither of the women, who lived next door, answered.

She became even more aware of the silence around her, a dead silence.

Alhaja is not dead.

She stood under the mango tree irresolutely. Then she remembered that the day was originally meant for Olori-Ebi's child naming ceremony, and lost all hope of getting help quickly. She knew everybody in the neighbourhood would be at Olori Ebi's house which was some distance away from theirs.

Moremi would have gone there if she knew the direction, gbómo-gbómo be damned, but her grandmother had been so protective of her, she had not been allowed to run around barefooted and sometimes, butt naked, like the other children on the street.

She walked dejectedly back to the main building and settled for standing guard in front of it. She would prevent Alhaja's soul from leaving the confines of the house.

"Why the shouting-shouting?" Iya Ruka rushed up to her, "I am hearing you from my shop,"

Moremi jumped off the ground and up in response, she nearly collided with Iya Ruka.
"What's the problem? Kí ló dé?" Iya Ruka steadied her.
"It's Alhaja, I can't wake her up, she is on the bed with her eyes wide open, please come and help me wake her." She tugged at the sleeves of Iya Ruka's blouse.
"Alhaja ke? Your grandmother?" another voice joined Iya Ruka.
Moremi narrowed her eyes at Iya Ruka's apprentice, annoyed at the way she was craning her neck as if she could see through the gloom of the passageway into Alhaja's room.
Iya Ruka grabbed the girl's face and turned it towards herself, "Run down to the clinic and fetch Matron, then go to Olori Ebi's house and tell him to come here immediately."
"Let's go and help Alhaja first," Moremi insisted.
"Do I look like a doctor or nurse in your eyes?" Iya Ruka snapped, she took a deep breath, gentled her tone and continued in Yoruba, "There's nothing I can do for her. Funmilayo will soon return with Matron who is in a better position to help."
Iya Ruka had just convinced her to sit down when the Matron appeared and entered the house without sparing a glance for Moremi. Olori Ebi soon followed after, in a flurry of neon green agbada and self-importance.
One hour later she watched, dry eyed, as Alhaja's corpse was washed and wrapped in readiness for her burial, which was to take place at sundown, according to Muslim rites.
Immediately Alhaja's body was lowered into the earth, from whence she came, the house was once again abuzz with activities in preparation for the ceremony to celebrate her life.
The first few days of the preparation for the post-burial ceremony was hectic, with people coming in and out of the house as casually as they did when she was still alive. Far flung relatives, most of whom Moremi had never seen before, turned up.
Olori Ebi, came only once, to lock up Alhaja's room and give an order that Moremi was not to be left alone. She noted that Olori Ebi was carrying two carton boxes overflowing with papers along with him.
The women agreed it would be wrong to leave the poor little girl

alone. And true to their words, they kept her company. They talked through her and about her, but none of them talked to her, well, except to ask her what she wanted for breakfast, lunch or dinner.

Moremi not only suffered through the invasion of her privacy in the days that followed, she also suffered a strange kind of oppression and a headache that was compounded by the constant wailing and whining of mourners that arrived from Alagbado the day after her grandmother's interment.

During this period she also acquired a patina of invisibility. This newly acquired superpower of hers manifested whenever she bumped into any of her relatives.

They would look at her, apparently surprised that she was there, their eyes would glaze over as their eyes sweep the compound, searching for more visible members of the family.

At the end of it all, she would remain standing at the exact spot while a steady stream of commiseraters patted her on the head, before rushing off to sympathize with someone of their social standing.

Moremi wandered around the compound in a confused daze, until she found herself seated next to the mourners on the third day.

Being professionals and used to seeing the dead and other invisible people, the mourners made room for her on the wooden bench.

They first studied her with caution, and then one of them asked who she was and when she told them they were at her grandmother's burial, they made mournful noises.

Their tears dried up a few seconds later, and they asked if she would be returning to England or America anytime soon. They did not listen when she told them she lived here, in Idi-Ikan.

People who looked like Moremi do not live in the heart of Ibadan, they lived at Bodija, or on the campus at the University of Ibadan. Posh places populated by the educated, the newly arrived from abroad, familiar strangers referred to as the àtòhúnrìnwá.

They told her how pretty she looked with skin so light and dark-green eyes, she was òyìnbó wasn't she?

They told her how shocked they were that she could speak Yoruba as sweetly as someone licking honey. They clasped their hands to their breasts and praised this achievement. Then they complained, rather

bitterly, about members of their own families who have refused to teach their children how to speak Yoruba. They listed the names of these criminals, careful not to leave any of them out.
"Ehen! See this small òyìnbó girl speaking Yoruba like a Yoruba person."
Their eyes were wide with marvel.
Moremi did not argue with them, she enjoyed not being invisible, she did not want to cause offense.
For the next few days she followed the mourners around and made certain interesting discoveries.
The mourners took turns crying, and that was why it appeared that they cried endlessly. They cried in batches, they had breakfast, lunch, dinner and snacks in-between, in batches.
Whenever a fresh face appeared in the compound, the women would begin wailing and singing Alhaja's panegyrics. Even while they cried, they laughed at jokes shared in low tones amongst themselves. Nobody paid any attention to the mourners, except to give them money or food.
But on the day of the burial, Moremi did not join the professional mourners, she wandered around the compound, a living ghost. She listened to conversations not meant for her ears.
Olori Ebi has bought six big cows!
Iya Sisi has left her husband for that her useless small boy.
The pots in the kitchen are not big enough, we need to get more from L'Egba.
Rabi is owing Iya L'Oja, you should have seen the fight! Rabi was disgraced well-well!
Moremi was sad, then she got angry. She watched, as they cooked and ate and pooped and laughed as if everything was fine. She watched as the women screamed and hugged one another, recounting stories of the last time they'd been together, at another birth, another burial, in another time, another space.

... of guardian demon

Tola woke up from a drug induced haze to the sound of a kitten crying persistently somewhere off to her right. She patted the bed, wondering how a kitten had gained entrance into the apartment. Something tugged at her memory but she turned her back on it, physically.

All she wanted was sleep... that's all...

She woke up a few minutes later, an hour ... a day?

The room was dark, the blanket warm, it smelt of her. A man came into the room, he helped her to sit up, he placed a mug in her hand, and she drank down the contents. It was pap; the tepid semi-solid paste wrapped itself around her taste buds sweetly-sour.

She accepted the pills and swallowed them with some more pap. She lay back on the bed, her brain was both tender and brittle, like it would shatter if she was not careful. She slid down carefully on the bed, her neck held stiffly. Head touched the pillow, the pillow was soft, fluffy, cloudy. The cloud wrapped itself around her brain, shielding it from danger, from shattering.

The kitten was shrieking. Tola frowned, she tightened the blanket around her head. Kittens shouldn't be allowed into bedrooms.

The next time she was awoken by a discomfort in her stomach.

She pushed the bedclothes off, the comforting, warm bedclothes that smelt like her unwashed body. As she swung her legs off the bed, a sharpened blade kind of pain, jabbed at her womb. She yelped.

The man who looked faintly familiar, like one of those faded black and white childhood pictures, stuck his head into the room, he stared at her for a while and then left.

She was relieved.

By the time she got to the bathroom, doubled over in pain, somebody was standing behind her. The woman, another faintly recognizable face, helped her to push open the door.

"Do you want to take a bath?"

Tola resented the woman's voice, she did not want to speak or be spoken to. The woman's voice demanded recognition, an acknowledgement.

"You should bathe," The woman's voice was a shriek, "you're smelling like a dead goat."
Tola's resentment for her grew. Ignoring the pain that jabbed at her insides, Tola pushed the woman away from the bathroom door and returned to bed. Sleep claimed her immediately, a dreamless, dead sleep.
The kitten is mewling again...damn it! The crying was coming from somewhere near her head. Her head started pounding.
Tola reluctantly dragged her lids apart, somebody was holding the kitten. The woman whose voice demanded recognition was back, she was thrusting the mewling kitten at her. She wondered why a kitten was all wrapped up in a baby blanket. She turned her head away from the woman and the kitten.
"Take your baby!" Commanded the woman, her voice ricocheted round Tola's brain, "You cannot continue to ignore him. You cannot refuse to breast feed him! What kind of mother are you?"
She pulled the blanket off her head and looked directly at the woman with hatred. The woman recoiled.
She shut her eyes and fell asleep.
The smell of something warm and tantalizing woke her up.
She opened her eyes and was met with a face full of worry. The face was light skinned. It wore a red lipstick, blue eye-shadow smoked up its lids. It smiled, showing pearly white teeth.
"Hey Tola, it's me Kemi," The face had a voice, a forced cheerful voice. "I'm your sister," she gave an embarrassed chuckle, "Remember me?"
Tola had taken a vow of forgetfulness, she was determined not to break that vow.
"Do you mind if I sit on the bed with you?"
She nodded, the woman sat down, just by her legs.
The woman fetched something from the ground. It was a tray, on it was a plate brimming with something brown and shiny, it smelt delicious.
"I brought you some fish peppersoup." The woman continued as she adjusted the tray so the soup would not spill.

As she scooped some of the peppersoup, Tola's mouth suddenly felt funny, like someone had lined her tongue with a thick layer of fur.

"Now open up," Kemi smiled encouragingly and pushed the spoon towards her.

She opened up, the spoon slid into her mouth, the peppersoup tasted as good as it smelt. She opened her mouth to receive another spoonful, then another...

"I told your husband that you might need to see a doctor," Kemi said as she scooped some more soup from the dish, "I think you might be suffering from post-partum depression. But your husband says being a GP means he knows everything about everything."

The peppersoup suddenly rushed from her stomach to her throat. She jumped out of bed and ran into the bathroom. She heaved until her stomach was empty.

Kemi was right behind her, patting her on the back, distracting her. Tola shrugged off her hand and went to rinse out her mouth in the sink. She ran some water over her head and wiped her face with a towel. Ignoring Kemi who was hovering behind her, she returned to the room, switched off the light, crawled back into her bed, swallowed two pills, and tuned out all the noise. She buried her nose in her armpits.

"Enough of this!" The woman was shrieking, "You have to take care of your husband and children!"

Tola cringed from her voice, from the words she was saying... of responsibilities, husbands, children...

"What's all these nonsense!" the woman was in full throttle, "You just gave birth to a baby! Are you the first person that will do operation to have a baby?" She leaned over the bed as Tola pulled the bedclothes over her head. "I am your mother! You will listen to me!" The bedclothes were yanked out of her hands, she was yanked out of bed. The C-Section wound protested by stabbing her with sharpened knives.

"Five weeks after your operation and you're still lying in bed, refusing to eat or breastfeed the baby! What kind of useless mother are you?" Tola's mother stabbed her with words as she pushed her towards the bathroom.

"Depression, what rubbish! Women have had children before you, they will keep having children after you're dead and gone! You will sit up and behave!"

Tola braced herself against the frame of the bathroom door, even though her legs were watery, she stood her ground and wouldn't budge when the woman pushed her.

"I want to be left alone," Tola jumped in surprise as her voice came out of her throat. She attempted to push her mother out of the doorway, but she was shoved back forcefully. As she fell down she hit her head on the toilet seat but the force was couched by the fake fur covering on the seat.

"I'm locking you in here until you come back to yourself!" Her mother yelled before slamming the door shut.

Tola curled up on the cool marble tiles of the bathroom floor and cried. The tears were drawn out of her aching womb. She cried harder because she did not know why she was crying. She cried until she started hiccupping, but she kept at it until there were no more tears.

"E don do, stand up." A soft, unfamiliar, voice said from somewhere above her head.

She pushed herself into a sitting position, but was too exhausted to ask the stranger who she was. How she got into a locked bathroom.

"I be Rita."

She looked at the woman properly. Although she couldn't gauge the woman's height from her position on the bathroom floor, the woman appeared to be really tall.

Her curves were emphasized by the red velcro mini-dress that clung to her body, white on rice. Tola couldn't make out her features.

"I be your guardian angel." The woman said.

She had an impression of black matted lips forming those words and sniggered; "Really? I've seen pictures of angels and none of them look like you."

Rita laughed, the sound travelled through Tola's body, "Okay, make we gree say I be your guardian demon." She leaned close to Tola, her face still out of focus, "I go take care of you."

She almost floated off the floor, she felt like air.

Gone was the boulder, the desire to curl into a tight ball and seek oblivion from sleep. Even the pains had receded.

She was born again ... old things have passed away, and behold all things have become new...

After she was done taking her bath, she knocked briskly on the bathroom door and the speed at which it was opened told her that her mother had been standing outside the bathroom all along.

She peered into the bathroom, "Who were you talking to?"

"None of your business!" Rita swept past her.

"Me?" Tola's mother hit her own chest, the sound echoed around the room. "You're talking to me like that? After all I've done for you?"

Rita stared at Tola's mother angrily, "I did not ask you to do anything for me. I did not ask to be born!"

a family that preys together

The meeting that would decide Moremi's fate was held in the parlour of Alhaja's house.

The parlour was the biggest room in the house. It had several old fashioned chairs, covered in forest green damask, spread around its rectangular shape.

The chairs were so immense one was led to believe giants had once occupied them, and that over the years their progeny had shrunk in size.

The walls of the room held sepia coloured pictures of long gone ancestors, whose spirits now occupy the white space, within the photographs.

The most imposing picture was that of Alhaji Alagbado, the family patriarch, Alhaja's great-grandfather.

It was positioned in a corner that faced the doorway.

Alhaji Alagbado was dressed in an agbada made of aso-oke, around his neck was a thick, gold necklace, with a huge pendant dangling off it. Both the necklace and pendant reached nearly to his ankles. On his right shoulder was a white saki, an insignia of the Ogboni Fraternity.

He was staring fiercely at the camera, as if daring it to imprint his face on mere paper, with mere chemicals.

The camera won.

For this important meeting, the parlour had been transformed into a community hall. The chairs that could be manoeuvred were piled one on top of the other, in different corners, while the heavier ones were pushed against the walls. Plastic chairs were arranged facing the direction of the only door that led into the room. Members of the family trickled in.

After a while someone shooed the children who were playing hide and seek, into the brilliant sunshine that flooded the courtyard.

As the room filled up, the noise level increased.

Moremi was dressed in an ill-fitting black gown, a gift from Iya Ruka, who had decided that none of her other clothes were appropriate for the occasion.

One is not dressed in t-shirts and jeans for mourning, and the few gowns she had were too brightly coloured.

Iya Ruka had brought the gown in that morning, freshly sewn on her own machine. The gown hung down to her toes, with no discernible waistline, although it bulged on one side and the short sleeves were tight around her armpits.

On Moremi's feet was a pair of black Cortina shoes that had been bought for her by her grandmother just before her death, the only thing that got a nod of approval from her self-appointed wardrobe monitor.

Moremi allowed Iya Ruka to drape her arm possessively around her shoulders as she was led into the room. Murmurs of sympathy rose from the people already seated.

Moremi and her temporary guardian slowed down as each person came to either assure her that she could call on them at any time, or simply patted her on the back. They told her in firm voices not to cry. *Crying will not bring back the dead.*

She nodded, she had no intention of crying, it was the visibility that bothered her. Somebody had snatched her cloak of invisibility off and she felt naked, vulnerable. She realized then that being ignored by her relatives was preferable to this obsequious performance of sympathy.

After a while, Moremi got tired of standing in the middle of the room – a thing to be pitied. She detached herself from Iya Ruka and walked to the darkest part of the sitting room, chose one of the chairs in a corner and squeezed herself into a tiny space. She pulled her cloak of invisibility around herself once again.

There was a flurry of neck craning as Morieba, a tall, dark skinned woman with ample breasts and neck draped in multiple gold chains, strode into the room.

She was dressed in a long-sleeved shirt and trousers made out of Ankara. She wore her hair in a low-cut, her face was blank, eyes shining with fury.

"Anti Morieba, you're back from London!" One of the women that had been hitherto gossiping with her neighbour shouted. She knelt down to greet Morieba, who pulled her up.

"Why didn't you call me when Alhaja died? Why did I have to hear it from some gossip that lives on my street?" Her baritone bounced round the room. "If you'd called me I would have gotten on the next flight out of London. I even missed the burial ceremony! I am particularly disappointed in you L'Egba, you have my London telephone number!"

"Don't be angry with me ma," L'Egba hurried after Morieba who had made a beeline for Moremi. "I tried to call you on the number you left with me at NITEL several times, but the telephone kept saying that something was wrong with something called a trunk."

Morieba pulled Moremi into a tight hug. Moremi struggled for breath amidst the heady perfume and enormous breasts. But she held on tightly to her grand-aunt, a little flicker of hope snaking its way into her chest. *Maybe things will be alright now that Aunty Morieba is here.*

"We will talk later," Morieba whispered and looked her in the eye. "You'll be fine." Moremi believed her.

As she turned to find a place to sit in the room, Morieba nearly bumped into Olori Ebi, who was closely followed by two of his sons.

Morieba and Olori Ebi ignored one another with an ease borne on the wings of long practice.
"Have you eaten this morning?" Olori Ebi planted himself in front of Moremi.
"Yes sir. Thank you, sir." She mumbled.
"Good girl."
His fatherly duties performed, Olori Ebi strutted back to the front of the room where a chair had been placed in readiness for him. His sons took up bodyguard positions on either side of the chair and glared at everybody.
The family ignored them and found seats, all the while exchanging news about the wonderful things happening to their children, and vicious gossip about family members that were not in the meeting.
The room fell silent as Olori Ebi rose to his full height. He was over six feet tall and had a girth to march his height. His tribal marks were deep and wide, they ran from the side of his head to both cheeks in the shape of L's, just like the one worn by his great-grandfather, who was also presiding over the room, through his photograph.
His triple chin trembled as he adjusted the abetí-ajá cap perched jauntily on his head, and in order to allow his subjects, also known as family members, enjoy the full glory of the pink jacquard lace, he stretched out his arms and swept his agbada gracefully back on his shoulders, in the classic 'one thousand, five hundred naira' gesture mastered by all affluent Yoruba men from the womb.
Olori Ebi had been the only male child Alhaja Aduke's father had. The fact that he was born in the patriarch's twilight years fed the family rumour mill that the old man's manhood wasn't what it should be. There was no way the old man could get it up, talk less of impregnating a nubile young woman.
Not one of them believed that Olori Ebi's real father wasn't Saka, the young teacher that had been posted to the village school around the time the family had married his mother.
Alhaja Aduke had fuelled this rumour during her lifetime, when she refused to give him more of the patriarch's property.
Olori Ebi cleared his throat.

The people responded with long and loud sucking of their teeth, which sounded rehearsed because of its perfect synchronisation.
He launched into a speech.
"We have all gathered here to execute a very painful duty. Death is a mean and vengeful master – "
He paused for effect. His inattentive audience took their cue and made sympathetic noises, hoping that would spur him to the point.
"It is the prayer of every parent that when they die their child will bury them, but it is not so in this case. Alhaja has one child, only one child and she is going around drinking cocaine, drinking heroine and having bastard children for unknown white men – "
He was interrupted by a screech from the back of the room.
Necks craned to see who was creating a scene. Scenes were good, they enlivened otherwise boring family meetings and provided fodder for gossip that could be milked for months and even years, if carefully managed.
"That is enough Olori Ebi! Please don't go there at all. It is only a dead man that knows those who will bury him!"
As soon as everybody identified the speaker they tried to keep their faces expressionless.
Morieba was not to be trifled with, at least not in her presence. She was a firebrand who had a two edged sword in place of a tongue, and was not afraid to use it.
She was one of Olori Ebi's nieces. Her mother had died at childbirth, and she had spent her childhood being shunted from one family member to another. She had been, *and still is*, as far as most members of the family were concerned, a bloody nuisance!
Always asking questions, always rocking the boat, always acting like a man! See how she's even dressed! Tueh!
It was Alhaja Aduke who had saved her from being the prostitute the family members suspected she would have become, when she took her in and set her up in a business.
Up till a few years earlier, she had been just another struggling woman selling 'provisions' in one of the biggest markets in Ibadan. Suddenly she became the richest woman in the family; even richer than Alhaja Aduke, her mentor.

and as it was to be expected, rumours floated round, about her, that she had used her womb for money-making rituals, that she was a drug dealer. The least favourite of rumour mongers was that she got lucky, when she got the sole distributorship of a new product which became an overnight success.
Fanciful people believed that it must be a combination of all three.
"Who is that fool that dares interrupt when I'm talking?" Olori Ebi barked. "Anyway, we are here to take a decision about what to do with Moremi. Who will take Moremi home? We have searched up and down for Alhaja's Will and the documents detailing her bank accounts and sundry, we are yet to find them. Which means there isn't a lot of money available, but I promise to personally support whoever takes this girl in with money from my own pocket."
Olori Ebi's words hung in the air for close to five minutes, and for the first time since the meeting was convened, silence reigned, nobody dared cough.
He fidgeted with his necklace and cleared his throat. Glanced at the doorway and continued, "I would have taken her in by myself, but as you well know, I have healthy sons in my house and I'd hate to cause temptation for my boys by putting a nubile, young..."
The words had barely left his lips when Morieba jumped off her chair, her breasts threatening to burst out of the confines of her shirt.
"Ehn Ehn! Olori Ebi! So you don't have any shame at all! How can you imagine that an eleven year old child will be tempting your boys? Something is really wrong with your brain. So you see a temptress in a child of eleven! Will you let me have her then? At least I won't need any of your stupid money to raise her."
Olori Ebi's face had become a mask of rage through her tirade.
"Not if you are the last person on the face of the earth!" He growled, "Rather than let a lousy and ill-brought up girl like you raise Moremi, I'd give her to a troop of monkeys!"
Morieba kissed her teeth, "How are we even sure you should be in charge of things sef? Where is Alhaja's Will?" She turned her wrath on other family members, she glared at each person in the room.
"And you're all going to sit down here and let this man bamboozle you with his jazz again! You're all going to keep quiet when he's

obviously lying about the missing Will. You will allow the fact that he's stuffed your mouth full of akara sold for one kobo, to stop you from telling the truth!"

None of them met her eyes.

She raised her face heavenwards, "Alhaja Aduke, the spirit of a mother does not sleep after death, do not sleep! Come and take revenge on your enemies!"

The room trembled, Morieba should know better than invoke the spirit of the freshly dead!

"A thousand dogs will eat that tongue of yours!" Olori Ebi thundered, "How dare you? Can you imagine this little child having the temerity to speak in the presence of her elders?"

His eyes were red, the veins on his neck stood out, his fists were bunched up.

"This is what happens when little girls have too much money, they become lippy! Who even invited you to this gathering?"

He stalked towards Morieba, there were noises of chairs being moved out of his way, but he didn't see them, he was Moses, his anger the rod that parted the Red Sea.

"Aren't you supposed to be out there with your mates playing with sand and wooden dolls?"

He loomed over her.

Morieba sprang out of her seat, snatched L'Egba's scarf off her head and wrapped it round her waist.

If it was war he wanted, she would give him one. She planted her feet apart, bracing herself like a sumo wrestler, held her arms akimbo, bounced on her toes, once, twice and launched herself at Olori Ebi – She had the tip of his parachute-like attire in her hands when strong arms restrained her and dragged her to the back of the room.

"Before we continue our deliberations please you should all take note of these ground rules."

He cleared his throat again and said calmly, "If you are unmarried, a suspected or known harlot and childless, you are not allowed to take Moremi home. It is only married and respectable people that can have her."

lakiriboto chronicles

He stared pointedly at Morieba as he threw the punches.
Hisses and hostile murmurs met his announcement. Still nobody spoke up.
"I will take her," ventured a man who had entered the room, while the fracas between Morieba and Olori Ebi had been brewing.
Necks were stretched again to see the person who had spoken. It was Kasali, Olori Ebi's second cousin. He worked at the Ministry of Transportation as a clerk, and was a well-respected man.
"Are you sure Kasali?"
Olori Ebi suddenly sounded stilted, as if he was reading out of a particularly badly written movie script.
"What will you do with her? You and your wife have already trained all your children, are you sure you want to start training this one too?"
"It is not me that will train her, remember Tola my last daughter? Doctor Wale's wife, well she just had another child..."
"Eeh e ku oriire o."
Voices congratulated him from all around the room. Mouths watered in anticipation of the feast that was sure to accompany this announcement. This was going to be one great month, two births and a death, food and aso-ebi galore, the women exchanged happy glances. Àríyá, the god of great Yoruba parties, had sprinkled gold dust on the family.
"She needs two people to help her with her household chores." Kasali continued as the voices died down, "I believe she and Moremi will deal well together. You know her husband is a doctor."
From Kasali's tone it was obvious that being the wife of a doctor was a very important position. It was a thing of shame not to have at least one doctor in the family, but Tola had saved them from shame by marrying one.
"Wait o!" Morieba was out of her chair again.
"So you want to take poor Moremi to your bratty daughter's house. The one that had three children in the space of four years! You want to turn Amope's daughter into a slave because her mum is not around and her grandmother is dead! You human beings are wicked! If you want a slave for your daughter, Kasali, go and look

elsewhere because I'm taking this girl home with me!"
She moved her chair out of the way and tried to return to Moremi but she found it hard going as chairs had mysteriously blocked her path and their occupants refused to budge even when she asked them to.

When it dawned on her that she would have to fight in order to take Moremi out of that room, she smiled grimly and shook her head.

She glared at them, but they all averted their faces, a self-conscious movement of the head.

"I've had it with you and your disrespect!" Olori Ebi started in triumphant tones. "Must you have an opinion about everything? For once in your life can't you just shut up?"

Yes! Good for her! The room murmured, nodding in time to the beat of connivance and duplicity that Olori Ebi was drumming.

"This is unacceptable behaviour and I will no longer stomach it. Little wonder no man has deigned to put you in his house. You are an unrepentant witch! Lekan! Kunle!"

Olori Ebi called his two sons who looked exactly like him, except where he had run to fat they were packed with muscles.

"Throw that woman out and don't let her back in here!"

The husky boys approached Morieba as they would a spitting cobra. Morieba stooped to pick her bag with unhurried grace, her body daring the boys to draw near her.

She sashayed towards Olori Ebi, stood in front of him, matching him foot for foot, her eyes trained on his.

"This is a seasonal film Raufu and this is just part one of season one." She moved closer to him and whispered. "You will not finish watching it!"

Olori Ebi's response was a smirk.

As she exited the room, the gathering burst into a round of applause – an overreaching woman had been put firmly back in her place.

... and another death

The night had been accompanied by a heavy rain that had lulled the village to sleep with its savage drumming, paving the way for a sunshine filled morning. The birds chirped busily at one another. The village square gradually filled up with communal goats, chickens and sundry domesticated animals, rumoured familiars of Alagbado's witches and warlocks.

A scream tore through the air scattering the animals that had been up all night (if rumours were to be believed) into different parts of the square.

Less than thirty seconds after the first person ran, helter-skelter, into Mogaji's compound, a crowd had gathered around Iya Kudirat. She was in the grip of a sadness so deep she left sympathizers bereft of words.

She looked so tragic sitting on the floor of their passageway that most of the women joined their voices to hers in heart rending wails as soon as they crossed the threshold.

The threads formerly wrapped around Iya Kudirat's hair, in pretty cornrows, were tangled together. Her blouse was torn and her wrapper askew.

She pulled the body of Isola to her bosom, the boy's head lolled back, his eyes staring into the netherworld.

"Isola! Isola! Answer me Isola! Please Isola!"

As she shook the boy's body his head flopped against her chest.

"Just answer me. Don't do this to me Isola! Aaah!" She wailed hoarsely.

Some men tried to take the boy from her but she held on tightly and growled at them.

"Leave her alone!"

Kudirat ran at the men head-butting one of them, she yanked at his trousers in an attempt to drag him off her mother. The man hit her with the back of his left hand without even glancing up. She yelped, stepped back and stumbled on someone's outstretched legs.

"Get out of here!" The man barked at her.

One of the weeping women helped Kudirat to her feet.

As she was being led out of the house, L'Egba ran into the passageway screaming like someone whose body had been drenched in hot oil. She tore off her scarf, tied it round her abundant waist, threw herself on the floor and started thrashing about.

Once again, L'Egba was in character as one who mourned louder than the bereaved. She was that peculiar relative who always turned up, when there was an urgent need for wailing and gnashing of teeth.

"Ori mi o! Aiye! Aiye mi o! Ori mi ti buru o!" L'Egba wailed as she rolled on the floor.

Her arms were wrapped round the head that she claimed has been destroyed by misfortune. She jerked around so violently that other sympathizers quickly moved out of her way before she did somebody bodily harm.

Iya Kudirat's head jerked up, her eyes, two chips of ice.

She wiped the tears off her cheeks and dropped Isola's lifeless body on the floor.

Before anybody could react, she'd pounced on L'Egba who, was still rolling on the floor, and started pummeling her.

"Witch!" She smacked L'egba across the face 'whack!'.

"You've eaten all my children."

Whack! Whack!

"When your poisoned womb can't produce boys why won't you go and kill mine? Today is the day you will meet your maker! When you get to hell, you can have a reunion with your dead mother who gave you witchcraft to eat!"

For a few minutes the crowd of spectators were frozen, not only at the way Iya Kudirat had attacked her co-wife, but at the methodical way she went about beating her up. The calmness in her voice, the almost soothing cadence of her violence.

"Stop it Iya Kudirat! Stop it now!" An authoritative voice rapped out from the crowd. The voice snapped the rest of the crowd out of their inertia and they turned referees, scrambling to be the first to separate the women.

Iya Kudirat, by that time, had sunk her teeth into L'Egba's neck, aiming for the jugular. L'Egba screamed continuously.

Kudirat stood by the door leading out of the passageway, arms akimbo. She shook her waist martially, nodded continually in satisfaction.

"That serves you right! Witch! You have finished eating all my mother's children, now it's time for you to be eaten!"

She rained half-understood curses down on the woman from the safety of the doorway. "Oloriburuku, Oloshi! You will never do well all the days of your life!"

A noise snagged her attention. She looked over her shoulder and caught sight of her father headed towards the house, whip in hand. His dark face rendered even darker by the fierce scowl on it. His tribal marks, stood out in relief against his cheeks. Sweat dripped off his face. He looked like the image of Satan the new pastor had been trying to paint for the villagers since he arrived at Alagbado to establish his church.

The last time her father looked like that, he had nearly killed the man who stole his pregnant nanny goat.

Kudirat knew that if she stepped out of the passageway it was likely she would be the first recipient of the whip her father was wielding, so she reentered the passage, jumped through the closest window and peered over the window sill.

She watched her father storm the passageway. She watched as he whipped her mother and L'Egba. She watched how people ran out of the house as speedily as they'd entered it earlier.

Her eyes were still locked on her father as he dropped the whip, picked up her brother's dead body and sat on one of the benches placed against the wall. Her heart thudded against her chest with the knowledge that he only had to look up to spot her, but she couldn't take her eyes off a man she could no longer recognize.

He was holding the corpse of her brother to his chest, the way he'd never held him when he had been alive, the way he'd never held her, lovingly, tenderly.

He buried his face in Isola's chest and wept.

She sat on the ground and joined her silent tears to his.

In the days that followed her brother's death, Kudirat kept her chatter to herself. She slept on a mat that had suddenly become empty. There was nobody putting their legs on her, pinching her, waking her up in the middle of the night demanding for water.

Isola's death had turned her mother into a shrivelled up woman who refused to sleep or eat.

Women of the village came into their home on silent feet. Whispers, sniffles and quiet sobs took the place of the cheery conversations that used to fill the house.

On the fifth day the heaviness became too much for Kudirat, she ventured out of the house and was soon deeply involved in the games played by the children who like her, were on holidays.

She and her friends had sat for their Common Entrance Exams the previous month, all of them waited anxiously for the news that they could proceed to the new secondary school the government had just built next to their primary school.

Kudirat loved school, she loved reading. She'd read the few books she'd found in the school 'library', a shelf full of worn books that she and a few others had read over and over until their covers had become tattered.

She wanted to meet with the children having adventures on English moors, those blond children on the cover of Famous Five books who seemed not to have any problems in the world except solving mysteries and eating gooseberry jam, scones and chocolates (whatever those were).

But her life was in this village, in a house that had become a shrine to her dead brother.

She waited for what she knew not, that life changing event she couldn't put a name to. Her anxieties peaked when she caught her father giving her furtive glances.

By the evening of the seventh day Kudirat was at the tip of screaming when her father summoned her into his room. He patted a space on his six spring bed, indicating that she should sit beside him.

"Kudi-Owo," he called her pet name.

She met his eyes then dropped them, remembering her mother's injunction never to look into the eyes of an adult. Things like that were pretty difficult for her. She mulled over her name as she studied her intertwined fingers. Kudi-Owo means 'bringer of wealth'. She did not think the name suited her because her parents did not have a lot of money. If they did, they would have bought that chocolate thing for her, they would have taken Isola to the hospital in Ibadan when he had started convulsing...

"I know that sometimes you think I'm a bad father," he continued.

Kudirat resisted the urge to look into his eyes again.

"But all the discipline I give you is because I want you to grow up to be a strong woman. The kind of woman that will make a success of her married life and have healthy, well-behaved sons and daughters for her husband." He paused as Kudirat's head jerked up, all attempts at not staring at him thrown to the wind.

Why is he talking about marriage and children?

Her heart thudded loudly in her ears. She yearned for so many things she could not name, marriage and children were definitely not on that list, even though she had no list. She'd never even thought of herself in those terms, she wanted to do... things.

Aren't I too young to be married gaan sef?

She swallowed the question when she remembered Birikisu, one of her friends in primary school. The girl had been married off as soon as she sprang a pair of breasts in primary five. For nearly three months, after Birikisu's wedding, Kudirat had tied a cloth round her chest, the gods forbid they start bouncing!

"I also want you to have a very good education." He interjected into her thoughts. "You know that these days whether you are a man or a woman and you don't have an education your life will be miserable. Look at Iya Wale, the village amebo, her problem is a lack of education. If she had gone to school like your mother did, she would have learnt how to mind her own business."

Kudirat's heartbeat slowed down, he was still talking about education.

Forgetting herself completely she relaxed and corrected that notion, because some of her teachers in the school were gossips and they were educated.

What has education got to do with being a gossip? It's either you were or you were not.

Kudirat's words dried up as her father's face gradually tightened.
"What I am trying to say is that, I have found a very good opportunity for you to make something of yourself. If you allow your head to rest in one place, you might even marry a doctor."
Baba Kudirat rose from his bed and shut the bedroom door, he threw open the windows in order to monitor passers-by.
Kudirat followed him around, "Doctor, Baami that one is a good thing! Everybody will be looking at me with respect. Everybody will call me Dr. Kudirat, just like Dr. Wale, Anti Tola's husband."
Kudirat's imagination took wings, there it was! That thing she wanted so badly. This was the opportunity she had been waiting for, a chance to get out of this small village. She would finally prove to her father that she was better than ten boys put together! Maybe she'd find out why her brother had died, why so many children die. And if she played her cards right, she might even go to London and eat that chocolate thing and scones and gooseberry jam.
Her father sat on the lone chair in his room, Kudirat knelt down beside him, "But before you can get to the point where you can marry a doctor, you have to work really hard and go to a good school. That is why I want to send you to Lagos so that you can live with Tola and her doctor husband."
Her father had barely finished talking when Kudirat leapt to her feet. What did it matter that her father thought she wanted to marry a doctor and not become one, she was going to live in LAGOS! The most beautiful place in the world! Lagos was filled with shiny things and shiny people. Everybody in Lagos was rich, they all drove big cars. Lagos was just a step away from London, all those oyinbo people would become her friend.
She danced a little jig.
That stupid Mulikat girl who had gone to spend one week in Ibadan during the last holiday had not allowed anybody to forget it. Every conversation she held with you was peppered with 'Ibadan this, Ibadan that', but she, Kudirat, was not going to a stupid Ibadan, she was going to live in Lagos – the richest city in the whole world, except for London.

According to the rumour mills, the chickens in Lagos were as big as houses, the tall houses were crafted from gold, there were a lot of bridges over the sea. She had seen pictures of the sea, it was big... the books said so.

Another thought then occurred to her, damming her joy.

"Baami, what about Maami? Who will help her around the house when I'm gone? Won't she be sad?"

"Don't worry about your mother Kudirat, I will handle her. Just go and pack your things, first thing tomorrow morning we will travel to Ibadan so that I can hand you over to Kasali who will then take you to Lagos."

Kudirat sighed and knelt down to thank her father, he placed a palm on her head, "As you are travelling to Lagos, do not forget the child of whom you are."

"Yes Baami," Kudirat made her voice as humble as she knew how, she even managed to lower her eyes. After the performance she jumped to her feet, ready to fling herself out of the door, to announce the good news to the whole world..

"And you are not to tell anybody about this." his voice stopped her, "Let them find out after you are gone. It's only the things done in secrecy that have any value."

Later that evening Kudirat was passing by her mother's room when she heard her parents talking in low tones, her mother sounded like she'd been crying. She paused and put her ear against the wooden door.

"It is for our safety. Didn't the pastor tell us she is a powerful Emèrè, that she's the one that blocked your womb? Remember he told us to remove her from our house or something calamitous would happen? Well Isola is dead. Do you want to spend the rest of your life as the woman who bore only one child, a female one for that matter! Let her go Abeni, let Kudirat go." Baba Kudirat said.

"But nobody in my lineage has ever been a slave to another." Kudirat's mother sounded outraged.

It was the first time in days that Kudirat would hear her mother's voice, she moved even closer to the door.

"You are saying I should send my daughter off to Lagos as a house girl. No, Baba Kudi, never!"

"Have you forgotten that she would be sent to school? Tola is a nice girl. She will never treat your child badly." Baba Kudirat's tone changed, "Let this girl go or you can both move to your father's house so that I can marry another wife!"

After her father's speech the room went quiet. Kudirat strained her ears but heard only the whisper of silence.

season 2
interesting times(2005-2007)

chief who is chief . . .

Olori Ebi's face was expressionless as he watched man and woman grovel before him. While they were telling him how magnanimous he was, he was thinking about the fickleness of human beings, their disloyalty.

He knew the couple too well, they were exactly like the others who had gone before them, men and women that had been in that same position at one point or the other, begging, singing his praises, but that was where it all ended.

They knew nothing about loyalty, they were pigeons, they would eat with you, drink with you, and as a matter of course, shit on you and then take-off in times of trouble.

"Olori Ebi, if you give us this loan, I promise to refund it to you as soon as the new shipment of my goods land."

The man's eyes were trained on him. "You know I've never asked anything of you before. But this is the only opportunity my son has to read law at the University of Ibadan. He is a very brilliant boy and we need just this fifty thousand naira to pay his registration fees and buy him a few things."

Olori Ebi also knew the boy in question and the boy was far from brilliant. Since he had started primary school, the boy had been notorious for repeating each class twice, how he had managed to pass his school certificate, (and so well!) baffled everyone.

In fact he and Kasali had a bet riding on the boy, that he would be expelled before finishing his secondary school education ... but since Eledua has made it a law that wonders should never cease in the land of the living ...

"... Tobi is a very good boy, I know he will never forget you if you do this for him, my in-law."

The kneeling woman's shrill voice grated on Olori Ebi's back teeth. He looked the woman fully in the face, and slowly hardened his eyes. The woman swallowed, shifted from one knee to another and finally dropped her eyes.

"Adele," each syllable of the man's name dropped like boulders off his lips. "If you were a woman, I'm sure you would be named 'Ruth of Moab'. I am surprised that a man of your stature would come to my house to beg for money and still be shameless enough to carry his wife with him."

He watched emotions chase themselves over Adele's face, from embarrassment to anger, the struggle that went on before the mask of politeness was firmly pulled back.

"I am sorry for bringing my wife along with me." Adele turned to his wife, "Mama Tobi, I think you should leave."

The woman rose off her knees without a word, her body held stiffly.

"Don't worry about that, it's already too late." Olori Ebi waved a dismissive hand. "It is men like you, who have no secrets from your wives and go around showing your lack of manliness that has given women the power to be talking back to other men. Anyway, how you run your household is none of my business. What is it to me if your wife wears the trousers?"

Adele shrivelled up at the insult. His wife remained suspended in motion, tears gathered in her eyes, Olori Ebi noted from underneath his bushy eyebrows that the woman did not allow the tears to flow down her cheeks. He grunted in disgust.

"I will consider giving you the loan, but as you both know, things are not as rosy in the country as they used to be and the farmland has not been yielding as much... but I will see what I can do for you. Send the boy to me tomorrow."

He waved them off, a pair of pesky flies.

Olori Ebi knew he would give them the loan. It was his role, his duty. He was the head of the family, the provider. The money would become what tens of other loans he'd made out to other members of his family, a bad debt, never to be paid back, never to be asked for.

Sometimes he resented the yoke of leadership the gods placed on his shoulder, but he would bear it. His ancestors had not gone around whining about family responsibilities; they had performed their roles without a second thought.

He would prove to the Alagbado family that he was a worthy son. Let them bring all their problems, he would solve every single one!

"Thank you sir, he will be here tomorrow," a subdued Adele answered as he rose from his supine position.

Olori Ebi dropped his head to his chest in pretend slumber and watched the couple troop out of the sitting room. He knew the two were going to start quarelling as soon as they got home, and that was enough. He chuckled.

As soon as they shut the door behind them, he lifted his head off his chest and sighed deeply.

What short memories people have! So Adele can come to me for money!

Adele's father was his uncle, (may Allah rest his soul). His father's immediate younger brother. The one that he had run to when he could no longer bear living in the village. In those days motor transportation had been scarce and expensive. Olori Ebi remembered the hard trek from Alagbado, to the man's house in Ibadan, his only companion the small bag full of boiled corn he had the foresight to steal from one of his stepmothers.

Adele's father had not even offered him a cup of water. He did not ask how he had made it to Ibadan. He had disregarded the fact that it was already after 6pm and ordered him back home.

That evening, a tired and hungry Olori Ebi had spent his first night in a motor park... the first of many... swearing revenge on everyone who had brought him to that point.

He looked up as the door to the sitting room was thrown open. Kasali bounced into the room in his usual ebullient fashion and started dancing as soon as his eyes lit on Olori Ebi.

He smiled genuinely for the first time on that hellish Saturday morning. It had been one dreary meeting after another, most of his visitors members of the extended family coming with their insatiable demands.

My wife is in the hospital. I need a job. My family has not eaten in two days. My children's school fees...

Not a single one of them had asked after his own pocket. How he made the money he doled out to them. How his immediate family were really doing. It was all about them.

Kasali was the only person who cared, the one man he could rely on. Kasali had never asked anything of him but friendship. He reminded Olori Ebi of his first and only dog, Bingo, that animal had been loyal to him. Kasali worshipped him, paid attention to every word that fell from his lips as if he was an oracle.

"Congratulations on executing such a great and wonderful family meeting Olori Ebi."

"The success belongs to both of us. That Morieba girl nearly ruined everything." Olori Ebi replied, magnanimous in victory.

"Ah, but you put her in her place Olori Ebi, right where she belongs," Kasali beamed.

"So when are you taking that child to Lagos?" He asked as soon as Kasali made himself comfortable on the chair next to his, "Doesn't your daughter need help again?"

Kasali looked uncomfortable. Olori Ebi's heart went out to him.

"How's Tola now? Don't you think we need to take her to see Baba Lalupon?"

"It's not me," Kasali frowned. "It's that husband of hers." He sighed dramatically. "He wouldn't even listen when I suggested that we should take her to see Baba, he said he's a doctor and a born-again Christian, that Jesus will take care of everything."

"Is that why you have not come to pick Moremi?"

"Actually no," Kasali was studying his interlocked fingers with the concentration of someone who would have to be examined on their length and width in a short while.

"Tola is much better now, in fact her mother has returned home. It's just that I think it's a good idea if I can find someone else to go along with her."

He brightened up and finally looked at Olori Ebi, "But I've been able to talk Baba Kudirat into giving me his daughter, she's presently at my place." His face fell again, "It's that son-in-law of mine, he said the timing has to be right, that he doesn't want me to just bring people to his house. He said Tola needs to be a little more stable."

lakiriboto chronicles

Olori Ebi moved to the edge of his seat, he nodded and made sympathetic noises. He sent a basketful of thanks to the gods who had blessed him with sons. He couldn't imagine how it felt having a child that might strip herself naked at any point and take to the market place.

Watching the dance of a madman is amusing, except the man is one's child.

"It's not that I'm pressurizing you, but I want Moremi out of Ibadan as soon as possible." He tried to get the urgency of the situation across to Kasali by gripping his arm. "I've been told that stupid Morieba woman visits the girl every day. I don't want her to influence the child with her wickedness or attempt to kidnap her. Please do this for me and you'll be adequately compensated."

"Haba Olori Ebi," Kasali pried his fingers off, "I'm not expecting anything from you, after all you're doing me a favour. Don't worry, I will take care of it. By the end of this week the girl should be in Lagos."

Olori Ebi stared at him a tad longer and suddenly flashed him a smile.

"Quadri!" He yelled as he pulled the door open. "Quadri!"

"Baami!" Quadri yelled in reply.

A thin boy of about fourteen, wearing a pair of glasses on his nose entered the room, an open book in his hands.

"Stupid boy! Oya put down that book. Go and bring me the half-bottle of Schnapps from my wardrobe." He handed Quadri the keys to his room.

"Yes sir," Quadri placed his book on the glass topped centre table and made to exit the room.

"Don't break it o! And don't drink out of it, I know the exact spot I left the schnapps!"

"Yes Baami," Quadri closed the door quietly behind him.

"You and these your sons." Kasali who had been delighted by the performance laughed.

"Don't mind them, all of them are drunkards," Olori Ebi sounded more proud than annoyed. "Anytime they lay their hands on my drinks they just finish it. One of them has been sneaking into my room, drinking my spirits and refilling the bottles with water. The day I catch the culprit ehn?"

i'm a very good girl ... father

Tola dragged herself out of bed... a chore as tasking as preparing Jesutitomi and Jesuwalaye for school. As exhausting as cooking... breathing itself had become a chore.
Her formerly slim body had thickened in the months that followed Jesulayomi's birth. Her breasts drooped heavily, her arms floated on the mass of fat that had accumulated underneath her armpits, her waistline thicker than how it had been when she had been pregnant. Her face was puffy and mottled with eczema and pimples.
Sloth, wanton, slut.
Traces of the beauty she had been at seventeen, when she was a spanking new bride, could be found in her thick lashes, her dark eyes, the tiny nose that sat between her high cheekbones.
Slattern, sluggard.
She had doubled in person, in personality. Tola had swallowed and birthed Rita and it showed in the stretch marks that mapped suffering on her stomach, arm and hips.
She drew open the window blind, the sight of the rutted road and filthy masses that passed along it like an army of ants, met her eyes. All those dirty, desperate looking people, always needy, demanding shit she did not have, from her with their eyes. They filled her with dread.
She shut her eyes against the images and took a deep breath. The stench of an open sewer filled her nostrils. She stepped back and closed the blinds.
As she turned away from the window the baby started screaming, she expelled an exasperated breath. He had been screaming all day, she tuned out the racket. It baffled her that people go on and have six or seven of them when she knew for a fact that she had three children too many.

All those people who go on about how beautiful babies were, their wonderful smell and so on and so forth should have their heads examined. Here she was praying for a few minutes of soul saving solitude, before visitors come banging on her door, and there he was screaming as if somebody had lit a fire under him.
He's been fed, diapered and watered, what else does he want from me?
His screams pierced through her mental block. She tried to focus on other things, but it seemed that the harder she tried, the louder he cried.
Smashing his head against a wall will be highly satisfying.
She ran into the room and stuck a pacifier in its mouth to stop it from driving her crazy.
Slipped into the toilet and fetched her stash of cigarettes from the tank. She lit the first one and drew the smoke inside her lungs, that first inhalation always hit the right spot. She welcomed the light-headedness that accompanied the smoke as it travelled down her lungs. She closed the lid of the toilet and sat down on top of it. Her shoulders drooped as she took another drag.
Tola wondered why people placed such ridiculous demands on her. They wanted her to marry, to have children, to be a slave, a lover, a good friend, to be supportive, to love her children unconditionally. She was supposed to be gracious, to be happy all the time.
She flicked cigarette ash on the tiled floor of the bathroom. Took another drag and rested her head on the toilet tank.
She wanted to be all those things so badly; she wanted to feel, to love her children. She wanted to genuinely experience that rush of love she had witnessed on people's face when they looked at their children. She had prodded and poked her insides but there was nothing but despair inside her. A deep darkness, hunger for something she had no words for.
How was she supposed to give what she does not have? Why do people insist on having children? Aren't there enough people on the miserable face of the earth to share the darkness therein?
The emptiness gnawed at her heart and she wanted to bawl her head off, to join her baby in crying at the unfairness of it all.

All I've ever asked for is freedom.
For a heartbeat she considered sliding to the floor of the toilet, curling up in despair and moaning till she felt better.
"Abeg stop am!" Rita, her guardian demon, materialized. "Wetin dey do this one? Wanting to cry, wanting to love... nyeh, nyeh, nyeh." She whined in a high falsetto.
"Who needs love? Dem dey carry am waka go market? Abeg light another cigarette–you go dey alright."
Tola lit up as she stared up at Rita, she had stopped wondering why Rita had no features.
"Ehn ehn, see how your bodi just cool. Make I come list the things I no understand, since this world is such a confusing place. I don't understand why you have three children, when you're obviously the worst mother in the world. I don't understand why you take all the bullshit that idiot you call a husband..."
"That's enough!" Tola jumped off the toilet seat, took a last drag of her cigarette and dropped the stub in the toilet.
She sprayed the room generously with a lavender air freshener and opened the windows to let the smoke out. She brushed past a giggling Rita into the children's bedroom. Grabbed the baby and looked into his eyes.
He cooed at her. *He is such a happy child, poor ignorant thing.*
"Just you wait." She whispered, "Wait for the world to snatch your innocence –"
She swallowed the rest of her tirade. *I won't be that kind of mother, it stops with me.*
She examined him thoroughly, as she'd done a hundred times before, as she'd examined her other children when they were babies.
He was the picture of health, with shiny eyes and chubby cheeks. Her father said he looked like her, she sincerely hoped that was not the case. He smiled at her toothlessly and she allowed him to curl his little fingers around her index finger. She smiled back at him and waited, no hoped, for that rush of tender feelings but nothing happened. She hurriedly fed him and changed his diaper. She patted his back gently until he gave a loud burp which made her smile... *smelly little thing.*

lakiriboto chronicles

She jumped as the bell to the flat rang.
"Who is it?" her fingers nervously flittered to her uncombed hair. She rushed to her room and pulled a comb through it while changing into a clean gown.
"It is us."
Her father's voice responded from the other side of the door. She was tempted to ask him who 'us' was but changed her mind. He wouldn't get it.
"I'm coming." She picked the baby up and then took her sweet time opening the door.
Her father was there with his ever present pleasant smile, his name suited him perfectly, Kasali Alagbado, Kasali the corn seller. A man of average height, he wore his pot-belly comfortably on his stocky frame. His eyes flashed merrily. Tola wondered how many shots of schnapps had gone into making him that happy.
Two girls cowered behind him. She forced a smile for her father and opened the door wider to let them in.
"E kaabo Baami," She sketched a kneeling to him as the three trooped into the sitting room. Her eyes widened as she took a closer look at the girls.
They are so young, too young to be placed in my care.
One of them was short, dark and slight. Everything about her was dainty. Her face was oval, her nose tiny and pointed, her mouth wide and smiley, her eyes danced with mischief. She reminded Tola of herself about that age; the only difference was that she looked happy, she couldn't remember the last time she'd been that happy.
The girl who stood beside her was tall and rangy, with disproportionately long arms and legs that put to mind stick insects. Her hair was a full mess of thick curls. Her mouth was wide, with a pair of full lips that looked as if they pouted a lot. She stared at Tola through a pair of wary green eyes, the other feature, besides her creamy skin which gave her away as bi-racial. The girls carried their worldly goods inside black polythene bags.
"You must be Baba Mogaji's daughter, Kudirat," She put as much warmth as she could into the smile, "and you," she took Moremi's limp hand in hers, "are Anti Amope's daughter, Moremi. I am

pleased to meet both of you. I hope we will all be happy living together."

"Yes ma." Kudirat said eagerly.

Moremi grunted something Tola couldn't catch.

"Please do sit down. I made some lunch because I know you guys will be hungry by the time you get here."

Tola said as her father made himself comfortable on one of the chairs. Kudirat made to take the baby from her.

"No, it's alright, you guys are tired, you will have more than enough time to carry him."

She turned a chilly smile on her father who had started pontificating about the names Nigerians gave their children.

"... can you imagine naming a child Moremi? You just stick the poor girl with a name that will stand out and probably embarrass her for the rest of her life. As if her white skin is not bad enough. What happened to solid names like Adeola, Amope, Feyisara, Isola and co? Some people don't even know what to name their children these days."

Without seeking her consent he grabbed the baby from her and tickled him. *Baami is not one for seeking consent.*

The baby giggled, and her father threw him in the air, he would catch him and toss him again. Tola felt apprehensive, the root cause of which she refused to examine.

"See me complaining to somebody who named her children Jesutitomi, Jesuwalaye and Jesulayomi." her father gave her a sly look from the corner of his eyes.

"Haba Daddy, you know I did not name the children by myself." She sat next to him, her eyes eagle sharp. "Left to me I will call them by the nice solid names you gave them - Tope, Asake and Femi. But I am just a woman, what rights do I have?"

"All these Kiriyo people just give names to children without checking if it will suit the head of the child it is being given to..." Her father continued, he had an audience now.

She ignored him and switched her attention to the girls who were still cowering near the doorway.

"Let me show you girls to your room and then we will have lunch." She grabbed the baby out of his arms. "After Daddy leaves I will show you around. My husband has arranged for a nice school for you just around the corner, you will start on Monday."
She showed them a room just off the kitchen. The room was very small but she had put in shelves and hangers for their clothes, a carpet and a fan.
The mattress was on the floor, it was covered by a blue bed sheet, a pink duvet was folded on top of the sheet. She remembered how lost and lonely she had felt when Wale first brought her to Lagos, she did not want the girls to feel unwanted or lost, that was why she'd gone out of her way to make their room as comfortable as possible. Sometimes she wondered at herself.
She studied the two girls closely. Kudirat was obviously pleased but Moremi's face was shuttered, although her eyes darted from one end of the room to the other, Tola could almost spot the curling of the tips of her lips.
She'd heard a lot about Moremi, how spoilt and surly she was, it appeared the reports were true. She remembered her mother referring to Moremi as emèrè, a wood spirit who'd been sent to the world to torture the Alagbado family by Karishika, Queen of the Underworld. Tola was determined to like the girl, anybody whom her mother disproved of must be an interesting person.
They moved to the kitchen and she showed them where the plates and cutlery were. She started dishing the food.
"I like your house," Kudirat broke the silence.
."Why, thank you Kudirat," Tola was genuinely surprised at the compliment. She tried to look at her house through her eyes, but all she could see was the puke orange and green that had been used to paint the flat inside out, Wale had chosen the colours, specifically, she suspected, to annoy her.
Her mother had also told her about Kudirat, whose only failing appeared to be that she was raised in a bush village that couldn't even boast of a major road. Her mother had described the girl in terms of a workhorse. She'd been advised to keep her husband and all her worldly goods away from the girls when they eventually

arrived because all housemaids were stealers of 'wordly goods' and husbands.
I wish someone would steal Wale from me...
They settled down at the dining table and devoured the food.
Tola's father belched and scratched his crotch for good measure.
"So children, this is your new home, you must promise to make your aunty very happy," He rose from the dining table and stretched. "I don't want to hear of any bad thing happening between you and her. Tola is a very good girl and has never given us any trouble, that is why I know both of you will be happy here."
Yes, I'm a very good girl father...
Tola had reconciled herself to the condescending manner her father spoke to her. A dumb woman who has never done anything with her life. She was as delicate, and as useful, as a rose bush in the middle of a cassava farm.
"Girls please clear this place and wash everything in the kitchen sink."
Tola rose from the dining table, it was time to dismiss Kasali Alagbado.
"Tola, I know I don't have to lecture you about how to treat the girls." He resumed pontificating.
But you will, won't you?
"You have to hold them with a firm hand. But be kind, and feed them regularly."
I don't need to water them too?
"You know how children can be a handful, you just have to call me anytime they start acting up…"
Tola stared at him, deadpan, as he went on and on.
"…I have to leave now for a meeting in Ibadan, I promise to drop in once in a while to keep an eye on all of you."
Oh yes we need eyes kept on us since we can't take care of ourselves.
When Tola still did not say anything, he changed the subject.
"So how's your husband? I spoke to him on the telephone before we embarked on our journey."
"He's fine." Tola rose from the chair abruptly and threw the baby over her shoulder. She had no intention of discussing Wale with him,

he never listened anyway. "Just give me a minute."
She went to her bedroom and picked the envelope full of 500 naira notes Wale had told her to give her father that morning. It amused Tola no end that everybody assumed that just because her husband was a doctor, they had a lot of money. Nobody knew about her husband's cocaine habit or that they were living at the edge of bankruptcy. But she had learnt how to take care of herself, Rita had taught her how to siphon money from their joint account. She had opened another account in her own name and kept the money there.
"No take too much o! Small, small, a ten thousand naira here and there every week, you can withdraw larger amounts when you notice he's drinking more heavily than usual."
She returned to the sitting room and handed the envelope to her father. Her father's eyes lit up as he pulled out its contents and started counting. After a while his face fell.
"I thought he was going to leave me more than this."
She could almost touch his disappointment. She wore her best impression of surprise and dismay as she took the envelope back from him, pretending to count the money, "I'm sorry sir, but that's all he gave to me."
"Do you have anything for your mother?" He asked hesitantly. She turned a glassy eyed stare towards her father and lifted a hand towards her temple.
"Sorry, I'm so sorry..." Kasali backed away from her.
Since her mother left the house over two months earlier, she had refused to speak to her. Her throat closed up anytime someone mentioned her, even Kemi had given up on pleading with her to forgive their mother.
"Now that we have the girls here our expenses will increase..." Tola continued as if her father had not just ruined an already ruined day.
"I have told you that you needn't spend too much on them." He interrupted her, "Just register them in a government secondary school. They don't need to pay school fees."
"But there's no more free education, and we need to buy their school uniforms and textbooks." She said.

"Textbooks ke? You don't have to waste money on that one. Just buy them the basics, English and Maths, they can borrow the rest from their classmates."

She gave him her glassy eyed stare again as she returned the envelope, turned abruptly and made for the door.

"I thought Olori Ebi would have sent the money for Moremi's upkeep to his account," Kasali did not budge from his position in the centre of the sitting room.

Tola turned towards him, hand on the doorknob. "We just paid our house rent, you know how expensive that is, that's beside the fact that our children are also resuming in school, everything is expensive in Lagos." The crestfallen look on his face made her gentle her voice, "Things are not as easy as it looks Baami."

She made a mental note to withdraw some more money from the joint account before Wale blew it.

"It's alright. What about you? Don't you have anything for me?" He flicked his tongue over his lips, the way a snake would dart its tongue out to taste the air.

"Baami!" Tola's laughter rang false, even to her ears, "You know I don't have a job."

"But that has not stopped you from giving me something in the past." He whined... flick, flick, his tongue went again.

"Like I said earlier, things are much tighter now," Tola walked casually towards him, "and we are just managing," She reached out for his hand and gently, but firmly, dragged him through the door, "don't worry, once I have something I will send it to your account."

She pulled the door shut and ushered him down the flight of stairs, hand firmly planted on the small of his back.

She removed her hand when they got to the road that ran through the front of the house and hailed a taxi.

As she waved him off the tight knots in her stomach loosened.

doki oloye

It was a beautiful Saturday morning in Lagos. The sky was a bright orange, it shone merrily overhead covering everything it touched with its warm, golden fingers.

But, all its warmth and shine did nothing for Moremi as she washed soap suds out of another garment belonging to a child.

Does it belong to Jesutitomi, Jesuwalaye or Jesulayomi? Moremi could not have cared less.

The darkness in her heart rivalled the sun. It was made up of helplessness, frustration, tiredness and a sadness she had been unable to shake off since her first arrival in Lagos. Every single muscle on her face was pulled tightly into a frown. Today made it two years since she discovered her grandmother's stiff body in her bed. It was two years since she became a drudge. Alone, abandoned, unloved. Two years of learning to take care of herself, of growing up as fast as it was humanly possible, learning to live by her wits.

Instead of being allowed to celebrate this milestone by curling up in bed, a blanket drawn over her head and wallow in self-pity. Instead of being allowed to mourn all she had lost... she was seated in front of a mound of dirty clothes.

Scrubbing, scrubbing, scrubbing.

She scrubbed every morning; clothes, floors, walls, shoes. No breathing space, no leisure, every time she had a break it was taken surreptitiously. Her free moments continually interrupted by children nearly her age, they needed to be cleaned, to be comforted, to be fed, children who needed her attention because they couldn't get it from their parents.

I'm a child too! I'm just a child!

Her once soft and pink palms had hardened into a pad, the back of her hands were wrinkled like those of an ancient woman. Tears threatened, at every turn, to pour down her face, a cascade that would easily fill up the fabled fountain of tears located at the point where the earth met the heavens. But she embraced the coldness within and hardened up her heart.

She used to cry before, every night she would rock and rock and rock on the bed crying for the girl she used to be, the home she'd lost, her absent mother, for a former life where she had been the pampered grandchild of an old, indulgent woman. She would cry until Kudirat wrapped her in a tight embrace. Kudirat's breath warm against her neck, whispering strengthening words; we'll be fine, nothing lasts forever, we will survive this.

"You're still here Miss Slowcoach," Kudirat sauntered over to where she was washing. She was carrying two bucket full of washed clothes. She took a look at Moremi's face and immediately dropped them.

"Here, let me finish doing this for you."

She sat down beside Moremi on the bench and tried to push her aside.

"It's alright Kudirat, I'm nearly done washing them." Moremi's voice came out husky.

Kudirat looked at the mountain of dirty clothes and then at her, when she saw the pout on Moremi's lips, she shrugged and rose from the bench. She walked the short distance to the lines and started hanging out the clothes to dry.

Moremi concentrated on a dark green spot and scrubbed it.

In the early days, when she still had hope that something could still happen, in the days of her naiveté ... whenever she was washing or scrubbing, her fingers would turn red, then they would bleed. Kudirat would bring out her precious package of shea butter and rub it on them.

Just as she'd lost her hopes, her hands had lost their tenderness. Her muscles that used to ache every night, after she'd done the day's work, had toughened.

Morieba usually visited her anytime she was in Lagos, the last link to the life she used to know. She would bring a pile of books, chocolates, clothes and money for her. She would bring laughter and good memories of her grandmother.

The first time Morieba came to the house, Moremi's heart had nearly flown out of her chest, she thought she would be rescued from Lagos, that Morieba was her fairy godmother. But her aunt had

shaken her head as they descended the staircase.
"I'm so sorry Moremi, I don't want Olori Ebi's wahala." She'd said, avoiding Moremi's eyes. "It's good that you're living with a family, every child needs the steadiness of a family, with a male figure." She had looked at Moremi with eyes full of words her lips were not speaking, "You know I'm single and I don't plan to marry any time soon. I'm so sorry." She cleared her throat and continued in a firmer tone. "But once you're being maltreated, just call me."
The question was how to describe maltreatment, how do you form the words? Would you describe maltreatment as not being allowed to sit on the chairs? Not being allowed to sing or watch TV? Would you call it the invasion of your privacy, when a drunken Wale would burst into your room just after you'd taken your bath? What do you call it when Wale took the gifts your aunt brought for you?
Was maltreatment when Wale insisted that you scrubbed the kitchen floor, the bathrooms and toilet every morning? On your knees, the scrubbing brush held at 90 degrees. The muscles in your arms contracting painfully from the amount of pressure you applied to it, because it must be clean! A speck of dust found on the floor meant you had to do it all over again.
How do you put all these into words without sounding like a brat? Isn't this what other girls in my position do every day of their lives without complaining?
Tola was of course, an angel. She was the one that returned your gifts to you on the sly. The one who spoke to you like a human being. She would, on her good days, laugh with you, talk to you about the books you'd shared. She would tell you not to scrub the floor anytime Wale was on call, she would make you special meals, on her good days. But Tola also came with her burden of secrets ... *I should be used to secrets by now, mother taught me about keeping secrets, I'm a secret keeper.*
Moremi hardly ever permitted herself to think about those days, but they existed, her Peckham Days, as she'd labelled them and locked them away in a dark corner of her heart, the same way she helped Tola, ...no it's Rita, not Tola ... lock away her clothes and shoes and that penis shaped rubber thing...

But since she'd started living in Lagos, her Peckham days would no longer be denied. They took over the good memories of the years she spent with her grandmother.
Peckham had been dirty, it was hunger. Peckam was mummy dearest telling you to hide in the wardrobe anytime someone came to the door, to keep quiet and listen to the creak-creak of the bed. It was wearing extra layers of clothes underneath your own clothes, inside the dressing room of big departmental stores, when you went 'shopping'.
It was when mummy dearest dropped little bars of chocolate, necklaces and wristwatches in your pocket and your heart would be beating like a drum because mummy dearest had told you that you had to smile your prettiest smile for the uniformed man at the door, so he wouldn't search your pockets.
Peckham was the day you were arrested by the man at the door, taken into a room and shown a video of yourself, while mummy dearest sniffled into her sleeves.
It was being taken away from mummy dearest and having to live with a bunch of other little children and a strange white woman who looked at you with eyes full of pity.
For a heartbeat she thought she would choke on air, that she would die from breathing.
She threw the cloth she was washing on the ground and stomped on it, she tore at it. When she heard that ripping sound, something in her lightened. So she took another one and ripped it into two and another one...
She could breathe better by the time she heard the snap of buttons popping off a shirt. She looked at the work her hands had wrought, a small heap of torn clothes were glaring at her from the ground. She nearly felt guilty.
"Hey slowcoach!" Kudirat was back, "nice work." She nodded at the pile of torn clothes.
"It's slowpoke not slowcoach!" Moremi snapped at her.
"Whatever," she shrugged. "Grammar no be my language."
She dragged a low stool in front of Moremi and started rinsing out the clothes in a huge plastic bowl.

lakiriboto chronicles

"I wonder why Tola didn't allow you to go for your grandmother's remembrance ceremony." She squeezed out soap suds from a torn gown.

"I didn't want to go." Moremi muttered.

She hated it when Kudirat tried to draw her out, somehow the girl thought she could make things better by saying a lot of rubbish and sounding all knowing.

"Liar!" She chuckled, "You so wanted to go."

"No, seriously, I don't." Moremi turned cat-green eyes on her. "Olori Ebi said they are just frying akara and there is no point in me coming."

"But if Aunty Morieba had been around, I bet she would have insisted that you should be there even if they're only distributing cups of water."

Moremi shrugged and continued scrubbing. Within a few minutes the girls were spreading out the last of the clothes, both whole and torn, on the lines.

"Good morning your royal highnesses."

The girls froze as they heard 'his' voice, that voice that hit them harder than punches. He walked towards them, jangling his car keys threateningly. Doki Oloye, the chief doctor, was the name Kudirat had given him in their early days.

Wale was a man of average height, who would have been considered handsome if not for his perpetually red, rat like eyes and the bags underneath them. His fair skin was as smooth as a baby's bottom, testimonial to the fact that hard living had nothing to do with skin condition. His entire expression was lofty. He knew everything and he knew it. His lips were thin and cruel. They were often twisted into a sneer. He had started nurturing a pot-belly that made him look like a malnourished, pregnant goat.

Doki Oloye the Donkey, because of his sticky fingers that wandered all over your body. His perpetually hard cock, that he would find ways of rubbing against you, particularly when he was 'punishing' you.

Moremi grunted in disgust when she remembered the day he had cornered her in the short passageway that linked the master bedroom with the children's room. He'd stepped out of the bathroom directly into her path, without a word he'd grabbed her hand and forced it towards the cock, "rub it!" he'd growled into her ear. She had stubbornly refused to... what stupidity is that? Rub what?

A silent struggle had ensued, with Wale trying to force her hand towards the cock, and Moremi resisting with all her might.

She'd been saved by Kudirat who had burst onto the scene and inserted herself between them, shouting for the neighbours at the top of her lungs.

Of course they'd gotten punished for it.

After that day she'd started carrying a sharp knife around with her, she swore to use it on him if he so much as smiled at her again.

"So this is what you do instead of doing your chores?" He continued, the girls stared at the ground and genuflected to him.

"Good moring sah," the girls spoke in the worst English they could muster because he hated it when they spoke good English to him, often meeting their words with a mocking laughter and a 'what do we have here? The queen of England herself', then he would tear the sentence apart, pointing out their grammatical errors.

Wale took pleasure in humiliating them. He would deny them meals or force them to eat leftovers when he felt offended.

He would mock Kudirat's Alagbado accent, whereby she replaced 'ch' with 'sh'. Kudirat had worked hard to get rid of the accent, but still slipped into it whenever she was upset.

"Will you get out of this place?" He yelled at the girls as they scrambled to clear the buckets and sundry things they'd been using for their laundry.

He stalked off towards the staircase that led to the flat, "I want breakfast and I want it now!"

Moremi made to rush after him but was held back by Kudirat.

"Where do you think you're going?"

"Where do you think I am going?" She frowned.

"Calm down Moremi." Kudirat folded her arms across her chest.

"You can't be going around fearing someone just because..."

"Moremi! Kudirat!" Wale was back, "Why are you still standing there?"
"Yessah! We her comin sah! We are a pack the buckets ni sah!" Kudirat responded in a sing-song voice.
Moremi had once compared him to Olori Ebi, the one symbol of darkness and evil in her life.
"Wale is not like Olori Ebi at all." Kudirat had said. "Olori Ebi is a hawk that would snatch a chick from underneath its mother's nose, but Wale is a vulture, a bottom feeder, he is the henchman that's always getting shot in movies."
"Don't let me have to call you again!" Wale shouted and left as abruptly as he'd appeared.
They rushed upstairs. After cleaning up and preparing some boiled yam and fish stew, they took out their portion first and hid it in their room, then they kept the rest of the food in the warmer and dished Wale's food.
Kudirat spat into the stew and stirred it with her fingers, the way Ngozi had shown them when they'd been holding one of the 'house-girls meeting' at the public tap, where they usually congregated in the evenings, ostensibly to fetch water.
The house-girls meeting was better than ten schools combined. It was where they shared tips on how to steal money without being detected. How to spit into the food of your mean bosses, the appropriate amount of spittle, or if you're daring enough, urine that would not show up in the taste of the food. How to deal with brats making your day horrible. Where to find the cheapest foodstuff so you'd be able to make profit when you were sent to the market. It was where they learnt about cocks, and fucks, and sexing.
Wale was glued to CNN when they placed his food on the dining table. The girls hovered near the kitchen door as he ate the food. Moremi's face was pulled into a mask of disgust while Kudirat giggled quietly.
The housegirls had taught them how important it was to witness and enjoy the humiliation of their tyrants.

the cosmopolitan housemaids of lagos

Kudirat watched, through the corner of her eye, while pretending to read a book, as Moremi tiptoed to Tola's room. She pretended not to see the bundle of clothes underneath her arm, when she emerged a few minutes later and ran out of the flat.

She and Moremi had been lounging in the sitting room, reading some books borrowed from Wale's bookshelf. It was one of those stolen moments, when they got some other housemaid to babysit for them, when Moremi's phone started ringing.

She had come to recognize the look that crept up on Moremi's face, the one she wore whenever she felt she was being burdened. Her cheeks would flush red, her irises would deepen into a darker shade of green. Moremi couldn't keep a secret to save her life but Kudirat indulged her. She enjoyed knowing what was going on without letting on.

Three years of living with somebody is not a joke.

She was watching a fashion show on E!, when she heard heavy footsteps mounting the staircase.

Kudirat wondered why Moremi was returning home with Tola so early. She hopped off Wale's favorite chair, straightened the throw pillows and removed the books she and Moremi had been reading from the floor.

She had just made it into their small room, which had grown even smaller over the years, and shut the door, when she heard the front door being pushed open.

She wondered how badly damaged Tola was this time around.

"I need your help Kudirat," Moremi was in the room with her, her eyes brimming with tears.

"Oh god, what has she done now?" Kudirat jumped off the mattress that Morieba had bought for them a few weeks earlier... after Kudirat had contrived to show her the flattened mattress they'd slept on for three years, while ostensibly giving her the recipe for her special melon seed soup with bush meat.

"Just come with me!"

Within a few minutes Kudirat and Moremi were in the bedroom with Tola. She was spread-eagled on the bed, moaning.

When she'd left earlier that morning, to go shopping, she had been wearing an iro and buba, with a headscarf, but the Tola that Moremi asked Kudirat to help her lift off the floor was wearing a body fitting red gown, with a deep neckline. The gown was stained with patches of dirt and blood. She had a small gash above her brow.

"Shouldn't we call Dr Wale?" The sight of blood sent panic screaming through Kudirat's system.

"Don't call him!" Tola slurred her words like someone who'd been at a huge quantity of spirits, in fact she reeked like she'd taken a bath in a whole tankful of ogogoro. Kudirat wondered where she could have gone.

Tola didn't have friends, and in the early days, she never used to go out except on the odd Sundays Dr Wale bothered to show up. But in the past one year she'd been going out regularly.

She would leave home in the morning, all happy and glowing, and sneak home in the evening. Moremi, the accomplice, ferrying mysterious bags up and down the staircase. Sometimes she would disappear for hours and return home, Tola in tow. After her outings Tola would suffer from depression for several days, refusing to come out of her bedroom.

Moremi stripped off her clothes, then she and Kudirat helped her into the bathroom. They turned on the shower and held her up. Moremi fetched some disinfectant and used cotton wool to wipe the wound on her head, the big scratch on her arm, the one near her ankle. After giving her a bath, they dragged her back to her room and helped her on with her nightgown, then they put her into bed.

"We have to go and get the children from Ngozi's place." Moremi said as they left Tola's room.

"You stay with her, I'll go."

Kudirat wandered out of the flat in a haze.

She was tired of living with the Roberts, bone tired. She was tired of having to look after children she was barely older than, tired of having to pick-up after them, clean their snotty noses, taking them to

school, entertaining them, chiding them and 'mothering' them. She wanted her mother too.
To think I'd been so happy when I was coming to live in Lagos.
She smiled as she remembered the girl she had been. The one clutching her dreams of the future along with a plastic bag full of her best clothes, the two careworn Nancy Drew novels she had inherited from her mother and her firm belief in the chickens of Lagos that were as tall as houses, of streets paved with gold, bridges built over an ocean that wrapped itself around the world like women wrapped their heads tightly with scarves.

In spite of it all she still held on to her dreams, that Lagos would smile on her and choose her as one of those special ones who made it. She would graduate as a medical doctor, that she would gain her independence.

When she had made straight A's in her JSS3 exams and everybody had been congratulating her, well... except for Wale who sneered and asked her what she thought she was doing passing so well, 'Are we getting ideas above our station?' She had laughed at all of them. She knew exactly what she had done, she had given the examination council what they wanted. She had a photographic memory and crammed everything that she was taught. All she did was replicate those words on paper. It had worked for her in primary school, it would see her through medical college. She wasn't in school to get an education, she got that from the streets.

She was soon at Ngozi's place, which was about five houses away from theirs, "Thanks for watching over the children." She said as the buxom girl threw open the door to their flat.

"Did you bring it?" Ngozi demanded, stretching her hand out.

She fetched a small bottle of oral contraceptives out of her pocket and placed it on her palm.

Kudirat got her education from girls like Ngozi.

Her madam's husband had been raping her since she resumed duty at their house as an 8 year old child. The previous year she had gotten pregnant and the man had taken her to have an abortion. She and Moremi had met Ngozi, the day after the procedure, when she had fainted at the public tap. The other girls had turned to them since

lakiriboto chronicles

they were the closest they would get to any kind of medical attention, after all they served a medical doctor.
Although they had not been of much help, except to give her some pain killers, when Ngozi had come round, she had been effusive in her thanks.
It was after that incidence that she had told them the story of her boss and his wife, who had turned a blind eye to what was taking place under her nose.
Kudirat was determined to help. Even if she could not prevent the rapes from happening, she would be able to stop pregnancies and abortions. So she decided to get her some contraceptives.
It had taken a lot of sneaking around, reading Wale's medical books and asking Tola seemingly innocent questions about reproduction. After a rather long-winded, and disjointed, lecture about the evils of sex, Tola had eventually shown them 'the pill' and where she kept them.
Kudirat supplied Ngozi with the pills, she stole them from Tola's bedside drawer.
"Thank you so much for these, ehn?" Ngozi said as she tucked the small bottle into her bra. "The work I am using them to do, you won't understand."
Kudirat narrowed her eyes at the girl, Ngozi was not to be trusted, "What kind of work do you use them for?"
Ngozi moved so close to Kudirat they were breathing in the same air. "I juss crush two of them," she jiggled her breasts, the pills shook in rhythm, "and put it into my Oga's food, the guy will just fall asleep like that! Piam!"
She stepped back and gave Kudirat a beatific smile that dimpled her cheeks, "Even now I no tink the man remember say I dey im house again, this ting, ehn? E better pass juju, those medicine people get better juju!"
Kudirat's face folded into a frown, "I don't understand, they are contraceptives, not sleeping pills. And why would you give it to your Oga instead of using it yourself?"
Ngozi's face shuttered, "Shebi it's that I don't pregnant again." She snapped.

She then grabbed Kudirat and steered her towards the room where the children were making a racket. She stopped and faced Kudirat, "This ting you give me, Oga don dey sleep well-well, no sexing, no pregnant."
She winked at Kudirat, who stepped back nervously, she would never want to get on Ngozi's wrong side. She suddenly turned serious, clapped twice and the children froze.
"The three Jesu's, prepare to dey go your house! But first, we dey come!" She commanded the children who looked at her in fear and trepidation. She dragged a baffled Kudirat through the passageway, through the kitchen, to the backyard.
"Wait here," she dropped Kudirat's arm and ran to the adjoining flat. She peeped through a window, "Esther, Esther, oya come!"
Kudirat watched the drama from afar. The tiptoeing, the closing of doors quietly, the whispers.
She had met Esther the week before, at the public tap. The girl was a new housemaid, a tiny thing that reminded her of the way she used to be when she'd newly arrived in Lagos.
"Ehn, ehn, this is the Kudirat I tell you about," She pulled the girl towards Kudirat, "tell am." Esther twisted her fingers and stared at her feet.
"Should I tell am?" Esther nodded.
"The ting is you know Sylvester nah, the boy that lives with Esther's madam."
Kudirat tried to recollect the boy, but failed, she nodded anyway.
"He sex Esther last night. She too she want the medicine. I give her one today so that the boy will leave her, but she want her own and I cannot be sharing the small one you're giving me."
Kudirat wondered if it was expected that once you were a housemaid you would also become a sex toy for all the men around you.
Her mother had taught her well, about men that liked little girls, about how to make sure they never come near her.
"They don't like you Kudi-Owo. They like power. They want to control you and your body, they want to own you." Her mother had turned away from the open fire on which she had been cooking on

that day and trained a hard look at her. "Anytime a man says that you should come and enter his room, just smile well-well and tell them you want to go and bring your mummy."
Kudirat missed her mum so badly at that moment, on the heels of that feeling followed resentment.
She sighed and turned her attention back to the girl standing in front of her, eyes averted, shame stamped on her posture.
She touched the girl on the arm, and whispered, "I'm so sorry about the ting wey happen." She bent closer, " e nor be your fault, the shame na for the idiot wey sex you. I go soon bring something for you ehn? But is it still paining you down there?" Kudirat asked. The girl remained mute.
"I have give her paracetamol, it was really paining her this morning."
Kudirat thought about the girl till she got home, her mute embarrassment, her rape, like so many others.

season three
playing with esu's balls
(2008-2011)

underground spiritual games

Olori Ebi straightened up, spread his agbada out, and wore his most forbidding expression as the door was pushed open. His chest tightened at the sight of his niece, Morieba. She was dressed in her usual masculine garb, today it was a pair of jeans and an outsized t-shirt.
She brought a smell of foreign trips, expensive perfumes and wealth into the room. Her strides spoke of her self-confidence, something that always disconcerted him. Most people that came into his home usually had an air of diffidence around them, but not Morieba, she strutted around like a cock, except she was a hen. When she knelt down to greet him, the proper way it should be done, he felt slightly better.
"Good afternoon, sir."
He took note that she didn't stay long enough on her knees, but one couldn't expect too much of a girl like that. He'd asked himself several times why he disliked her so intensely, why her presence bothered him and made him uncomfortable, the only answer he came up with was, 'she talks back'.
He resented the easy way she wore affluence, the confidence in her stride. He resented the breath of her shoulders, the thickness of her arms. Her hair-cut, the car-keys dangling casually from her fingers, the way she sat, legs spread apart... *like a man!*
"I hope you and the boys are fine, sir?" She asked politely after making herself comfortable by the edge of the chair.

Olori Ebi grunted and leaned back on the chair, his fingers splayed across his mouth and nose, his eyes watchful, wary.

"I met Iyawo on my way in, she's looking really well Egbon mi, you're taking..."

"Stop there! Just stop it!" He barked, jerked up from his slouch and leaned towards her. "Why are you here? What do you want?"

Morieba bared her teeth at him in the parody of a smile, "I actually want you to listen to what I have to say, because I know how you switch off when you don't want to hear the truth."

Olori Ebi lifted his eyebrow at her last two words but he swallowed the bile that threatened to burst out of him and forced himself to relax. The truth, he wondered what she knew about those words, whose truth? Hers?

"I was in Lagos to see Moremi." She announced as if she'd done something miraculous, "Actually I had just returned from one of my business trips to India—"

He narrowed his eyes, "Young lady, do not come here with your ill-mannered boasts about world travel, we have heard. We know you went to India and China and Dubai and New-York, just tell me exactly what you want."

He saw quickening anger in Morieba's eyes and grinned inside. He loved a good fight, he loved when he had a worthy opponent. Morieba was one of the few worth crossing swords with.

"Why are you here?"

Morieba moved closer to the edge of her seat, but somehow managed not to wobble, or as Olori Ebi hoped, fall off. She made small growling noises in her throat and narrowed her eyes.

"I will never insult an ancient man like you, or else I would have considered your remark fuelled by jealousy. But since I'm a well-brought up woman who knows her own worth and does not cringe from bullies." She suddenly relaxed, "Don't let us quarrel Olori Ebi, you're like my father, you have done a lot for me," she paused, "Even if I do think you could have done more."

Olori Ebi shook his head, Moremi obviously hadn't learnt how wicked the world could be, she was about to find out.

"Alright, go on." He placed his elbows on the armrest of his chair and covered half his face with both hands.
"I have a business proposition for you." She started.
Every muscle in Olori Ebi's body listened, he sat up straighter and paid attention.
"I don't like the way Moremi and Kudirat are being treated in Lagos, I don't like it at all."
Olori Ebi did not move a muscle, she was beyond redemption.
"And I think it's more of Wale's fault than Tola's."
He wondered about her mental health, the way she switched from one emotion to another couldn't be normal.
"You should have seen them, particularly Moremi, her hands are red and raw from washing clothes, all her clothes are torn."
The more Morieba talked, the louder her voice became. She seemed to be in the grip of hysteria. He shook his head in sympathy ... poor child.
"I've bought several clothes for her in the past few years, but I don't think she's allowed to wear them. Her hair, my goodness! She's all skin and bones."
When she stopped talking, he waited for more, but she was taking deep breaths.
"Let me get this straight, you came here to tell me how Wale and Tola are maltreating Moremi."
"No Olori Ebi, it's more than that! Children should live with people that care about them. For one, I don't think Tola has totally recovered from the episode she suffered after having her last child, and Wale is the most irresponsible man I've ever seen. In the past three years I've been to their house more than twelve times, and I've never met him at home, not even once!"
He was truly baffled, *why are women like this?*
"Correct me if I'm wrong, but, are you saying that you expect Wale, who is a doctor, to be at home just because you're visiting?" He used his most reasonable tone, he wouldn't want to trigger her again.
"None of the things you're saying makes any sense, or is it that those children are telling you tales so you can feel sorry for them?"

Moremi expelled an impatient breath, "They've not told me anything! They don't need to tell me anything. I've been there, I've spent time with them! I saw them three days ago and spent about four hours with the girls. For the first two hours Tola didn't even bother to come out and say hello, and that's not the first time she'll be doing that. I eventually went inside her bedroom because the girls claimed she was indisposed, my goodness, it was horrible. The room stank like a gutter and Tola was in bed with clothes and shoes piled all around her, she wouldn't even say hello to me."

He tried to listen, especially to the things she wasn't saying, like jealousy, after all Morieba wasn't married and Tola was.

"... we need to sort that girl out! The most bizzare aspect of the visit happened when I was about to leave. Tola came out of the room, all dressed up and acted as if she had just discovered my presence in their house! We need to get those children away from her and get her away from that man! She needs to see a proper doctor!"

Olori Ebi held out placating hands, "Calm down madam! Firstly I don't know what 'episode' you're talking about. See, let's not get all confused." He sat back in his chair, "Let me understand this, you claim that Moremi and Kudirat are not being taken care of, yes?" Morieba nodded.

"You forget they were not sent to Lagos to be taken care of, they went there to learn about responsibility and hard work. You weren't raised by your parents were you? Neither was I. You didn't turn out too badly. Look at how far you've come due to hard work."

Olori Ebi was deliberately being obtuse, and he knew that she knew.

"Kudirat and Moremi are children!" Morieba's voice was pitched to the highest volume possible, and it grated on his nerves. "They shouldn't be made to take care of other people's children!"

Olori Ebi sucked his teeth. "I can now see what all these travelling up and down has done to your brain. Is Moremi the first person to go and live with other people? Have those other people died? And those girls are not children, aren't they in SS2 now? Some of their age-mates are already married with children sef!"

Morieba suddenly looked unsure of herself. He relaxed against his chair, he'd won another round.

"Okay, let me put it this way." Her voice jerked him out of his self-congratulatory mode.

"A few years ago, Alhaja and I went to her lawyer's office." Her voice was low and full of menace. "I was the other witness and I do have a rough idea of what is contained in the will." Her gaze commanded his to look into hers. "I will stop searching for Alhaja's Will, in fact I will not bother you about the Will again, if you let me have Moremi. I will personally hire a housekeeper for Tola and pay her a salary."

Olori Ebi was done with her nonsense. "I can see that you are not only stubborn you are also hard of hearing." He jumped out of his chair with an air of finality. "In one sentence you've made some veiled threats and at the same time you've tried to bribe me, with something you don't have!"

He towered over her, his agbada spread out like the wings of a hawk about to dive on a chick. "Listen to me very well. If your empty womb is crying for a child, I'm sorry but you can't have Moremi. Go and born your own! I know all your secrets Morieba, don't push me!"

He turned and pulled open the door, he was particularly proud of the way he swept his agbada after him. "By the way, good luck with finding the Will, haven't you been searching for it for the past four years or so? I'll be very happy when you do!"

He shut the sitting room door without another word and went directly to his room, pulled off his agbada, turned on the fan and sat at the foot of his bed.

Morieba, was a true Alagbado who never made idle threats. If she'd made up her mind to find the Will, that was exactly what she would do. He quickly climbed back down the stairs and met Iyawo shutting the front door.

"Aunty Morieba was really angry." She said as she turned the key in the lock. "I don't know why you people squabble like little children—"

"Nobody asked for your opinion!" Olori Ebi barked, "Go and get me some of the akara you fried this morning, and a bowl of palm-oil. Put them on that wooden tray and bring them to my room."

Iyawo stepped back, clasping her hands to her chest. "Sorry o, the owner of my bride wealth."

He sucked his teeth at her sarcastic tone, stomped back to his room and changed into something more comfortable.

By the time he had finished dressing in an ankara shirt and its matching trousers, Iyawo was knocking on his door. She placed the things he'd requested on a table and gave him a hard stare before leaving.

He slid his feet into a pair of rubber slippers and pulled open the toilet door. After locking it securely behind him, he grabbed the torch beside the toilet bowl, switched it on and balanced it carefully on the tray. He opened a smaller door that led out of the toilet into the older part of the house that had been sealed off years ago.

The house had been originally built by his great-grandfather who had raised it from a bungalow into a one storey building. His father had 'modernised' it by adding a new wing and using it as his base whenever he came to town from Alagbado.

As he transversed the passageway, the thin white light of the torch, periodically lit up the blackened mud walls, scampering rats, and thick dust motes that tickled the back of his throat.

He took a right turn and descended the rickety wooden staircase that led into the lower part of the building. He treaded carefully as the staircase shook alarmingly with each step he took and expelled an angry breath as he reached the bottom of the stairwell.

He resented that he had to make these pilgrimages, he had done nothing to be ashamed of, but that was the way things had to be. In the days of yore, you put your gods out in the sun, displayed their beauty for everyone to see. There were constant sacrifices and annual celebrations of your family gods. You proudly bore their names, you were Esubiyi, Sangowanwa, you were Oyafunmi, Oosagbemi. But the imported religions and their fanatics had put an end to all that.

You had to hide your worship of the gods so nobody would call you evil. You had to blend with the crowd, as the days of tolerance were long gone.

Those days that you could be an Ogun devotee and a chaplain at the same time. Nowadays, anything relating to ancestor veneration was viewed with a large degree of suspicion. No longer could the Imam

carry his father's Egungun, you were either one or the other. So you took your gods underground and worshipped them on the sly.
Olori Ebi placed the tray in front of the Ibeji carvings mounting guard to the shrine that had been in the family from time before history. He crouched in front of the statues and offered each one the akara, all the while chanting their panygernics:
Ejìre ará-ìsokún edúnjobí
Omo edun tíí ns'eré orí igi
Ófese méjèèjì bo sílé alákìísa;
Òsalákìísà d'onígba aso
Accept this sacrifice and let the ears of the gods be attentive to my petitions.
He rose to his feet, dusted off his clothes and entered into an even darker room. He switched off the torch and reached out for a clay lamp seated just above the door post, took a box of matches off the post and lit the wicker.
The lamp flickered its orange flames casting long shadows against the walls and the statues of the gods.
He stepped further into the room, and made for the statue of Èsù seated in the left-hand corner. He placed the oil lamp on the ground and lifted the clay pot full of palm oil off the tray. He dribbled the oil on the statue's head and knelt down in front of the messenger of the gods.
Láároye
Adíjààle ta'kété Bàbá òríta
A fi'bi díre, a fire díbi
Má se mi o
Má so béèni mi di bééko
Má so bééko mi di bééni
"Láároye, I've brought evil reports of Morieba, the daughter of Oluronbi to you. Morieba came into my house to threaten me! After eating my pepper and oil, she had the guts to come into my own home and threaten me!"
Sweat dripped down Olori Ebi's back so intense was his anger. His voice bounced off the walls into Èsù's ears.
"There's no hiding the truth from you because you're the all-seeing one. Aduke the daughter of Ajoke was the one who first stole my

inheritance. Instead of allowing me to take charge when I came of age, the woman called me a criminal and gave me two buildings and a piece of land deep inside one bush village to shut my mouth. I had to send her to an early grave because it is the person who asks us how we will complete our tasks that we show how it is done.

Instead of leaving 'well-enough' alone, her apprentice, Morieba, the daughter of Oluronbi has threatened to go and search for a Will that I have decided has to remain missing, just because she wants the custody of Moremi, Aduke's granddaughter."

As Èsù fully apparated in a room filled with the smell of ancient offerings and heartfelt pleas, they allowed themselves to soak in the history of the people that had created them for the Alagbado lineage. After a while they studied the young man sweating so passionately in front of the soapstone statue that represented them and reflected on how they used to be annoyed with the way people kept conflating them with the European Satan. But these days they only found being thought to be what they were not very amusing, mischief making had just been made easier. After permitting themselves a faint smile, they paid attention to the things the young man was not saying.

Olori Ebi paused to catch his breath, the room had grown stuffier than it had been earlier, he was sweating from every pore of his skin. He used the hem of his shirt to wipe his face.

"Here is my errand, and here is the palm-oil." He dribbled some more palm oil on the statue. "I want you to dodge Morieba's footsteps with all manner of ills. I want you to make sure disfavour and ill-will follows her around. That she will be so busy with all the trouble you will visit upon her, she won't have time to go about searching for stupid Wills. That you, Onileorita, Ologiri Oko, will dodge her footsteps with illnesses and disease, That her business will fail and she'd turn destitute. And if she persists, I want her to die! Yes Èsù, I want her to die a sudden death, the same way her mentor died! I am ready to pay any price you demand of me, just do as you have been told and do it within the week! Ase!"

Olori Ebi felt lighter as he put off the lamp and climbed the staircase back into his room.

He fell into a deep sleep as soon as he hit his bed, only to be woken up by a loud hammering on his door.

"Baami! Baami!"

"You are a big fool!" Olori Ebi yelled as soon as he pulled open his door, "How dare you come to my door and start shouting like the house is on fire? Haven't I told you that you are not to come near this room except you have been summoned? Answer me Lekan!"

"Baami I'm sorry, but I have important news." The boy mumbled.

"By Ogun, I hope the news is important enough or I will skin you alive!"

"It is Baba Kasali sir, Tola just phoned now, she said he's dead, he was involved in a car accident..."

't' for trouble

"Oyinbo, come and cut the grass over here!" Mr Hakeem beckoned at Moremi.

Back in her grandmother's house she'd not been aware of the difference between her and other children in the neighbourhood.

She knew she was special, but it wasn't because of her skin, she had been special back then because she had toys and her grandmother loved her. That had changed when she moved to Lagos. In Lagos she acquired a new cognomen, 'oyinbo', but more than that she was treated with a combination of disdain and fascination, but she was always treated differently.

It had gotten worse as she grew older, her skin, defying her refusal to apply any kind of cream on it, shone as if the sun itself had taken refuge underneath it. She'd grown taller, her outsized arms and knobbly knees finally catching up with the rest of her body. Her breasts were small and perfectly rounded, her stomach flat, hips as slim as that of a young boy.

She'd been told by many, both strangers and people she was familiar with, that she was beautiful, she should become a model. Moremi didn't want beauty. Beauty was a burden she refused to bear. She'd

rather have Kudirat's melanin, her shiny, blue-black skin that bestowed belonging, anonymity, and a beauty that had nothing to do with the colour of her skin.
She did not want to be an exotic species, a thing to be placed on a pedestal, something not totally human.
"I'm talking to you Moremi!" Mr Hakeem snapped.
She stood to attention.
"Me sir?"
She heard muffled laughter from her classmates. They had learnt over the years that she never answered to 'oyinbo'. She arranged her features into disinterest and sauntered, as slowly as she dared, over to where he was standing, all six foot of him. Mr. Hakeem was a tall drink of water, who has been drunk, and drunk.
Mr Hakeem was well built and had boyish good looks which he complemented by a well-groomed beard. Mr Hakeem was a believer, he believed he was god's gift to all the girls in Bariga Comprehensive High School, and maybe he was. For it appeared that he didn't have problems bedding both teachers and students. According to the rumour mill.
"Just one kiss," He whispered as she drew close to him, "Not even a kiss, one peck, and you can return to your classroom."
Moremi was not in the least surprised, she'd heard worse pick-up lines from people who didn't even have the tenous claim of familiarity that Mr Hakeem could, because they sometimes crossed paths on the school corridors. But she had also been well tutored by Kudirat, and sometimes she ad-libbed.
"I can't hear you sir," Moremi said calmly as she took a step back from him. "Can you speak louder?"
"Come on, don't be stubborn," He whined close to her ear, bringing to mind mosquitoes singing her their malaria song while they prepared needle sharp proboscis to feast on her blood. "You know I love you, I want to even marry you."
"Mr Hakeem sir!" She pitched at the highest volume possible, even as she took another step away from his invasion of her space. "You still haven't shown me the patch of grass I'm supposed to cut sir! If

you point it out I'll be able to see it sir! Because I can't hear what you're saying sir!"

"You really are as arrogant as everybody says you are," he hissed, "So because you're oyinbo, a broke one at that, who is even a housemaid, you still go around with your shoulders raised up."

Moremi gave him her trade-in-mark dead-pan stare, "Where did you say I should cut sir?" Her voice was a solid wall of ice.

When Mr. Hakeem realized that he wasn't getting anywhere with her, he growled and pointed at a dense bush as far away from the others as possible.

"Thank you sir!" Moremi shouted. Her classmates, who had been pretending all along to be so interested in cutting grass that they hadn't been enjoying their bit of afternoon entertainment, tittered.

Moremi approached the grass cutting with the same dedication, total concentration and intensity she applied to doing her household chores. Her long arm brought down the machete on the grass with precision, each time she raised it up, it would flash in the midday sun like Ogun's avenging machine.

She soon developed a rhythm, accompanied by a long stream of curses which Èsù thoroughly approved of.

Èsù was on an evidence gathering trip, examining the life and times of the Alagbados in the story Olori Ebi had shared with them. Not that they weren't familiar with the Alagbado clan, but they'd lost interest in that lineage since they had stopped asking for their intervention. So far Èsù approved of all the women they'd been asked to visit.

Moremi had run out of steam and was deep in conversation with her classmates when bell for closing hours rang. They filed to the staff room and discovered that Mr. Hakeem had left some hours earlier. She dropped her machete in the storeroom and went to wait for Kudirat at the school-gate.

She should be mad at Kudirat because it was her fault that every single girl in SS3 had been punished, all because of hairstyles. But she wasn't, she was amused.

Moremi didn't have any problems with her hair, she had a problem with the hairdresser, a middle-aged woman who was rather fond of shoving their heads in-between her thighs, the stink of her badly bleached skin nearly choking her to death, while she gave her hard knocks if Moremi so much as moved her head to breathe in some clean air. One day she'd headed for the barber's and had it cut as low as possible. Although Wale had told her how ugly she looked when she got home, Moremi knew that it was one of the best decisions she had ever made.

Kudirat on the other hand loved her long, thick, hair. She cared for it as a mother would a new-born baby. She wore it in beautiful styles, during the holidays and on weekends, she would condition it with shea butter and coconut oil. She would comb it until it floated, nimbus like, on her head. She and the hairdresser had a mutual admiration society going on. The hairdresser plaited her hair lovingly, and she claimed that inhaling the stink of her skin was a small price to pay for a heedful of beautifully plaited hair.

Kudirat had always resented the way the school dictated hairstyles to the students. She hated it more because erring students were punished by cutting off any hairdo that did not comply with their dictates, with a blunt pair of scissors. She had one of her brilliant ideas on the day a girl was given a shave on school assembly, the JSS1 girl had been blubbering, tears of humiliation and snot running down her face.

Kudirat had launched a campaign amongst the SS2 students. She told them how unfair the school policy was, how it was humiliating, and why couldn't the girls wear any hairstyle they wanted as long as it was kept clean and neatly done. There had to be a protest, a mass thing that would shock the school authorities.

After a series of meetings, the girls had decided that on Monday they would wear their hairstyles differently from whatever style that was dictated by the authorities.

Moremi had participated in all the meetings, barely able to keep her amusement to herself, she thought the girls would not have the liver to push through, she had underestimated the resentment for authority that hid in the hearts of 15 year olds.

She had been surprised to discover that every single girl in their grade that did not wear their hair in low-cuts came on that Monday with their hair either floating freely on their heads, like Kudirat had done, or woven into tiny complicated styles that had the school authorities calling an emergency meeting. The result of that meeting had been their punishment. Kudirat and the other ringleaders had been carted off to receive special punishment from the principal, while Mr. Hakeem had been delegated to mete out punishment to the minions.

Moremi waited for nearly one hour, before an exhausted Kudirat, with clothes stained and awry showed up. Her eyes were puffy and red from crying.

"We were made to cut some elephant grass at the back of the junior classes with blunt cutlasses." She answered Moremi's unasked question. "Then she got Mr Shaba to cane us."

She displayed the raw bruises on her palms to Moremi. Moremi grabbed the bruised hands and made to kiss them.

"Idiot, get away from me!" Kudirat pushed her away playfully.

"You stink!" Moremi announced gleefully.

"So do you, Miss Ring o' ring o' roses. That's not all." Kudirat pulled a neatly folded paper out of her pocket and handed it to Moremi, who quickly scanned through it, wincing at the typos.

"What is this?? You have to bring our parents to school tomorrow morning or you will face expulsion."

"Yes... so how has your day been?" Kudirat asked in a false cheerful tone.

Moremi shrugged, "Not as bad as yours, at least the grass we got to cut was not elephant grass, our machetes were rather sharp and I also got a marriage proposal."

"Mr Hakeem!" Kudirat burst into laughter, "You lucky girl, you."

"You don't know how lucky I am." She was deadpan. "After marrying my broke-ass teacher, I will never do another day of work in my life, except maybe cook, wash and bear many many children... by getting sexed every single night."

The girls stood dead in the middle of the walkway and laughed, they leaned into each other and laughed so hard tears were streaming down their faces. They laughed so loudly that other pedestrians gave them a wide berth, while some kind bus conductors yelled directions to Yaba Psychiatrist Hospital, to them.

"Is this how we are going to spend the rest of our lives?" Kudirat hiccupped.

"How else are we to live? We are expected to spend our entire lives dodging penises and drudgery. It's why we were born, what we were born to do. We are girls, we shall not be sexed!"

That thought sobered them up faster than a bucket of cold water. They crossed the road, and embarked on the final lap of the trek that would take them to their street.

"You are in deep shit though."

Kudirat curtsied, "Thanks for that piece of wisdom oh great one."

Moremi ignored her tone and continued, "Tola is out, we might get home now and she'd be in her room with the windows and doors barred."

"Or she might have gone to one of her ogogoro joints and is getting ready to call you to come and rescue her." Kudirat added sneakily.

Moremi eyeballed her and sucked her teeth loudly, then continued talking.

"Wale is hardly ever at home, and even if he is, he'd not go to your school out of spite, which you'd be thankful for, because if he does, he'd not only get you expelled," she giggled, "he'd also have your name stricken off the school register."

"It seems," Kudirat mimicked Wale's deep tones, "we are getting ideas above our station, aren't we, your royal highness?"

Moremi suddenly remembered Ortega, one of their classmates, she smiled "I have an idea though, how much are you carrying on you?"

Aside from the money they stole from both Tola and Wale, the girls were making a brisk business with the Housemaids Cabal (as Kudirat referred to Ngozi and her gang). Ngozi had suggested that instead of just giving the pills away they should make some profit from it. Housemaids from as far as Ikoyi were now patronizing them, buying the oral contraceptives as quickly as they could steal them.

Wale supplied the medicine, they supplied Ngozi with the pills, she supplied her chain of housemaids and remitted their cut to them. Everybody was happy.

Although the girls seemed to be using the pills all wrong, the important thing was Ngozi and her friends were no longer getting sexed.

"How much do you have?" Moremi asked.

Kudirat rifled through her pinafore pocket and pulled out a wad of notes, "I found about 10,000 naira in Doki Oloye's pockets yesterday when Tola asked me to do the laundry."

"Good, give me 5k and follow me." Moremi stretched out her hand to receive the money, and turned towards the seedier part of their neighbourhood.

"Where are we going?" Kudirat asked apprehensively.

"We are going to see Ortega," Moremi replied as she jumped over the huge gutter that separated them from relative safety.

"So Moremi, when did you become friends with Ortega?" She snatched her hand out of Moremi's "When did you start keeping secrets from me?"

"Ortega and I are not friends." Moremi snapped.

"How did you know the way to his house?" Kudirat sounded jealous.

Moremi did not say anything, she had no intention of telling Kudirat that she'd been to fetch Tola from a beer-parlour in that part of the neighbourhood several times. She looked Kudirat in the eye, "If you don't want to go we can always turn back, after all it's your problem not mine."

Kudirat glared at her, "My problems are yours."

Ortega was the toughest and roughest boy in their school. Whenever somebody was being bullied or a mean prank was being played on a teacher, he was to be found leading the pack. Rumour had it that he smoked weed with a bunch of other miscreants behind the boys toilet, during school hours. Moremi knew it was no rumour, but Ortega not only smoked the weed, he sold it alongside other hallucinogens that helped students cope with their messed up lives. It was no wonder that he hadn't been expelled from the school but hedged his bets, selling drugs to the teachers, and helping them to 'leak' exam papers.

The girls walked past houses built so closely to one another that the space between them was non-existent. Most of them were unpainted and the ones that were, had faded to a filthy version of their original colours. The houses looked dejected, as if they were well aware of their condition.

After 5 minutes of dodging laundry hung out in the sun to dry, open sewers and other things best left unexamined, they finally slowed down in front of a ramshackle aluminium building which, incongruously, had a cable television dish hung on one of its outer walls.

Moremi was still wondering where she should knock when Ortega came out of the room, and used the ratty curtain that hung on the door to cover his body.

"Hi Ortega," she said brightly. "It's me, Moremi."

"And so what?" Ortega sneered, "The great white girl has come to visit the poor black boy so we should throw a party."

"Ortega why now? Wetin I take do you wey you dey behave like this? I wan ask why you no come school today."

"Why you like to dey ask those kind questions? How he take consine you whether I go school or I no go school, you be my mother?" he scowled at them. "How you take know my house sef?"

"Don't be like that Ortega." Moremi wasn't surprised at his hostility, the last time they had spoken he had asked her out and she'd turned him down.

"I get better deal for you. At least come outside so we fit yarn better thing. I no come here with dry mouth o."

She dipped her hand inside the pocket of her school uniform and brought out a wad of 100 naira notes.

Ortega quickly dragged her inside the house, Kudirat at her heels.

"You should never wave money around like that in this neighbourhood. We nor dey joke at all!"

After delivering the short lecture, he turned on the light and a naked bulb flooded the room with brilliant yellow. The room was a perfect square with a queen-sized bed that took up most of the space, a couch was placed alongside one of the walls and directly in front of it, just above the bed, was a shelf on which sat a huge television set.

Beside the couch was a cupboard on top of which was a stove, on which was a pot. Ortega picked up a faded blue t-shirt draped over a chair and covered his bony chest with it.

"I have a job for you," Moremi plunged into the silence, "and we will pay you very well. We need to rent parents for Kudirat tomorrow. Tell them to dress nicely but not too nicely. They have to convince the principal not to expel Kudirat. I will give you an envelope tomorrow morning which you'll give to her. I am sure she won't do anything further to Kudirat after she gets a bribe."

"No lele Moremi," Ortega's eyes filled up with mischief, his earlier hostility melted in the sun of naira notes, "you know say that be my job. Kudirat's parents go dey the school gate tomorrow morning." He turned to face Kudirat, "Make sure you come in early so that you can get to meet them before you go in."

"Okay, thanks." Kudirat mumbled and shifted from one foot to another.

"How much you go collect?" Moremi went to the heart of the matter.

"The parents will take 15,000 naira and me I go collect 5,000 naira finder's fee."

"Don't be silly, 7,500k each for just 30minutes work? Lai lai, even sex worker nor dey cost reach that." Moremi pulled out the money from her pocket, "Let's do this quickly. I will pay Mr and Mrs Mogaji, five thousand naira each and pay you three thousand naira finder's fee."

Ortega accepted the cash and counted it, "Wey the balance?"

"After dem complete their work successfully."

"Moremi baby, the only Moremi that ever liveth. Paddy mi!"

"But you were calling me names earlier!" She snapped.

"You know as e dey go nah," he sobered up, "I'm sorry, I shouldn't have."

"It's alright," She smiled at him. "I know say anybody wey give you money na im be your best friend, until you've finished spending it."

"You know that's how I roll." His voice took on a bus conductor's gruffness.

"Don't forget the name, Mr and Mrs Mogaji." Moremi said as they stepped out of the room, Ortega wrote the name on a piece of paper.

The following morning. Kudirat's parents turned up at the gate as

promised. The man and woman looked like they were in their middle ages and wore matching Ankara outfits. The woman was plump and smiley, the man thin and stern looking.
Moremi's respect for them grew as she watched Kudirat enter their class looking properly humbled and sad. The illusion was dispelled as soon as Kudirat passed by her table and flashed a saucy smile.
"Did you notice that they didn't cut anybody's hair? We won!"
Her whispered words lingered with Moremi all through that day.

the sleepwalker...

Tola knew the exact moment Wale rose from the bed. She knew this because his side of the bed suddenly became lighter. She knew this because he had been getting up from her side regularly for a whole week and she would follow him with her mind, eyes tightly shut.
He would first go to the sitting room, walk around for a while, he would go to the kitchen and open the fridge, he never shut it, he would then head for the toilet, and finally the children's room.
After a whole week of following him with her mind and studying the patterns of his midnight wanderings, she had gone to the children's room and peered at him through a crack in the door, because he had stayed in there for longer than usual.
He had been standing still at the foot of the bed the three Jesu's shared. He had leaned over and placed gentle kisses on the children's foreheads. He had straightened the rumpled bed sheet, covered them with their bed clothes and adjusted pillows.
On the surface, he looked like a caring father, but she knew him better than that, she knew he couldn't be trusted, not around children.
Wale cared for nobody, not even for himself. He was a pleasure seeker who did whatever it took to get him high at the moment he wanted it. He was also smart and cunning; he groomed his victims until they were willing slaves to whatever depravity he had in mind.

In fact she had thought all that had ended when one of their neighbours had confronted him, claiming that he had made her little child fondle his penis. There had been a lot of shouting and denials, but things had gotten so bad they had been forced to move from Ikoyi to Bariga.
He's turned his attention to the children.
The possibilities were horrifying, reminding her of her own childhood, uncles with groping fingers; uncles that wanted you sitting on their laps, uncles kissing you on the lips, warning you to tell nobody.
No one was going to do that to her children, it would be over her dead body.
In all their years together, when she'd pretended not to see how he touched Moremi and Kudirat, it had never occurred to her that he would eventually do that to his own daughter.
The following night, Tola pretended to be asleep, she jumped out of bed when she thought she heard whimpers and burst into the children's room, Wale straightened and rose from the children's bed. Jesutitofunmi's nightgown was scrunched around her waist, her pant pulled down to her thighs.
Wale brushed past her without a word. She sat in the space Wale just vacated and straightened her daughter's clothes, when she was finally able to look up, her eyes met those of Jesutitofumi, they were full of fright.
Tola's tummy turned water.
"Daddy was touching me, I told him to stop," she whispered.
Tola wept as she lifted her daughter out of the bed and carried her into the sitting room. With trembling arms she pulled Jesutitofumi into a hug, her daughter's tears soaking through her gown. After a while, her daughter's trembling subsided, so did hers, so did their tears.
"Has he touched you before?" She whispered the question that had been on her mind for over a week.
"Yes," Jesutitofumi replied, "he puts his tongue in my mouth. He said I shouldn't tell anybody, that he loves only me."

Tola's stomach churned, her throat closed up with revulsion at what she'd allowed to happen, but she pulled herself together.
This is not about you Tola!
Tola waited a while, but Jesutitofumi did not say anything further, she pulled away from her and tilted her face upwards.
"He will never touch you again, I promise you that." She said firmly, more to the voice asking her how she planned to stop Wale, than to her daughter.
The pain that thrust itself into Tola's heart as she realised that her daughter was staring back at her with a mixture of mistrust and fear, was so deep her chest contracted.
She scrambled around for something to say, anything that would soothe her daughter, a desperate need to earn her trust.
"I will protect you, I promise, I won't let him hurt you again..."
Tola knew she was babbling but didn't know what to say. She wasn't prepared for this.
There was no handbook to guide her, no one prepared her for this. No one told her what to do in case her children's father decides to assault his own children, what could she say?
She felt a movement against her shoulder, Jesutitofumi was saying something.
"What did you say?" Tola pulled her daughter's head off her shoulder.
"Is it true that you're mad mummy?" Her daughter asked earnestly, her eyes begging Tola to say 'no'. "Daddy said you have mentallo, he said your head is not correct and that is why he loves only me."
Tola froze and tried to answer that question, am I mad?
"Yes I am," Tola's voice wobbled as she admitted the truth, "I am mad, Jesutitofunmi." Her voice grew firmer, "But your daddy is madder, his madness incurable, he should be locked away."
"That's what Kudirat said too," Jesutitofunmi whispered.
Tola wanted to howl, to let out the pain that was tearing at her insides. She didn't, she had to feel the pain, to let it eat at her so she would never forget this moment. Her pain would be a marker, it would serve as a memorial of the living horror she'd put her daughter through.

"I don't care if you're mad!" Jesutitofumi said fiercely, "I love you mummy."

Tola rocked Jesutitofumi until she slept off. For once she shut down the demons, all the voices were banished. For once she would listen to her daughter's heartbeat, she would listen.

In the early hours, when she heard Wale moving about in the master's bedroom, she returned Jesutitofumi into her room and went to the kitchen.

Still quiet inside she fetched some beans and started the process that would turn it into akara.

She poured herself into the preparations, peeling, blending and frying the bean paste. She whipped up the pap in no time and had the dining table set by the time Wale emerged from their room, all dressed up.

It was 4:30am.

She nodded at the table and watched him sit down. Still without a word she sat across from him and waited until he'd taken a bite of the akara before speaking.

"Why are you such a bastard?" Her tone was conversational, almost casual. "In the paedophile's bible I guess there's no such thing as incest."

Wale considered himself to be poker faced, but Tola had lived with him long enough to recognize the little signs. A flicker of something akin to panic skittered through his eyes before the cunning took over.

"I don't know what you're talking about," he shrugged.

"I saw you in the children's room last night and Jesutitofumi told me it wasn't your first time of sexually assaulting her." She choked the words out of a mouth that was dry with fear, words that became real, solid. She wanted to flee from that table, reverse the hands of time so she wouldn't have to be in her present position.

"I don't know what you are talking about." He paused, frowned a little, and then continued with his meal.

After taking about three spoonful of pap, he realised that Tola's gaze was still on him, he looked at her again, "Maybe I was sleepwalking.

I am known to sleepwalk on certain occasions, under certain circumstances."
He returned to his meal.
"I never knew you sleepwalked," she said softly.
"You know nothing my dear wife, so let's just keep it like that." He gave her his most charming smile and dropped his spoon. "How are you sure about the things you claim to see? Are we sitting at the dining table? Are you holding a conversation with me or one of your imaginary friends? You know your delicate condition Tola, your tendency to see things, to hear voices. Am I even in this flat?".
He left his side of the table and leaned close to her, his lips hovered over hers. Bile climbed up her throat as her world was filled with those lips, the things they could do to her.
"Calm the fuck down baby," He whispered. "What you need to do at this point is what you usually do, watch African Magic and drink vodka," his voice became a growl, "don't fuck with shit you can't handle!"
He straightened his tie, gave her a contemptuous look and turned to leave.
Tola's head went burst, she saw red.
Her voice, the one that had been silenced since she got married to him at barely 17years of age, burst through the barriers that had been imposed on it.
Barriers imposed by her mother's voice telling her that a woman should do everything in her power to keep her marriage; of the church telling her that she was the neck, her husband the head; of the society telling her that divorced women were the whores of the earth; the voice of her insecurity about her mental health...
"I have taken a lot of shit from you Olawale Roberts."
Rita's voice blocked his path. It was a thing of marvel, this loud voice of hers, Wale had no choice but to turn in order to see the woman that had created it.
"I know how you mess around with little children."
Wale opened and closed his mouth like a fish that had been taken out of water. For once his dead-pan, seen-it-all mask had fallen off, in its

place was amazement.

"Don't fucking mess with my children again." She walked up to him. "You can mess with my head, finger my brain, but if I catch you touching any of my children again, you won't live to regret it!"

Wale grabbed her shirt, "Did you just threaten me?" He yelled. "Did you just say you're going to murder me if I touch my own children?" A look of cunning look entered his eyes and he gentled his voice, "So I should not play with my own children again. I do hope you listen to yourself Tola, I've been telling you that you're totally bonkers, totally. All these years I've helped you to hide your shame by not having you committed to an asylum. I help manage your sickness, I supply you with meds, but all you do is..."

Rita grabbed his shirt in a strong grip, "Meds Wale, what meds have you been giving me? You've been giving me meds without my knowledge?"

Before she could say anything further Wale sent her head spinning with an open palm slap, pushed her away from him, and slammed his way out of the flat.

Tola lay on the floor for a while, refusing to give in to tears. She pulled herself off the floor and entered her bedroom, she shut the door after her, she began to hyperventilate.

I nor know why you nor wan make I take care of this bastard!

"No!" Tola said firmly.

She'd experienced Rita's method of 'taking care' of things. It usually involved Rita doing things Tola couldn't remember, things that led to her having wounds all over her body or getting stuck in strange neighbourhoods and having to call Moremi to come and pick her in a taxi.

Things that involved high heeled shoes, short gowns, dark rooms, strange men that smelt like dirt and sweat.

Things she wouldn't even want to recollect. Things that were best left behind in dark, dangerous rooms, stuffed into polythene bags by Moremi and hidden away in dark, dangerous cupboards located somewhere in the kitchen.

Who will believe me? Who can I call?

Tola's hand shook as she dialled Kemi's number. Her older sister picked it up after the first ring.

"Hello Tola, how are you? This is a pleasant surprise!"

The words got stuck in her throat. Where should she start from? Would Kemi even believe her?

She'd never been close to her sister, not even during their childhood. Especially not after her episodes started at the age of 8, when she would refuse to sleep, eat or go to school for days. She couldn't find the words, they were too descriptive, too shaming, so she settled for the conventional lie.

"I'm fine. I just thought it's been too long since I spoke to you."

"How are your children and husband?"

"Fine, they are all fine."

She was saved from having to tell more lies when the doorbell rang, "Kemi, let me call you back, someone's at the door."

Her heart sank as she pulled open the door to Morieba.

She had never particularly liked the woman who walked through her door as though she owned the house, but then she'd never particularly disliked her either.

She'd never been particular. She was Tola, your friendly neighbourhood 'not particularly' woman.

She glanced at the clock, it was 5:45am.

"Good morning anti Morieba." She was careful to place an emphasis on the 'morning'.

"I'll go wake the children up." Tola bared her teeth.

"No please, not yet," Morieba did not return the smile. "I came to talk to you."

Tola didn't feel like talking to anybody, she had enough problems of her own. She wanted to go into the bedroom and close everybody out. She wanted a smoke and a shot or two of vodka.

Nobody cared about what she felt like anyway, so she sat down. It was an activity that was normal. Normal people sat down, they don't hover, or growl no matter how hard they wanted to. They don't yell at visitors, they sat, down.

There was also a little guilt, one of the reasons she felt uncomfortable in Morieba's presence. She had forgotten a lot of things about her childhood, but not Morieba as the teenager who came to live with them around the time Tola had started her episodes.

She remembered the shameful manner her parents had treated Morieba before she was eventually sent away for being too headstrong.

She felt somehow responsible for her parents bad behaviour.

"Can I get you something to drink ma?" She asked politely, finally breaking the silence that stretched out between them, a silence full of unspoken words, resentment, shame and embarrassment.

Morieba shook her head. "We need to talk." She patted a space beside her, "would you mind coming closer?"

Tola shifted a little closer to her, wondering why the woman was being so dramatic.

"I am sorry if in the past I made you to feel as if it's your fault your parents treated me less than human when I came to live with you guys."

Morieba was well known to be tactless so Tola was not surprised by her words.

"It was not your fault, you had nothing to do with it. I know that you have your own problems, but I want to talk to you as a woman, and a mother." Morieba raised her hands and smiled ruefully. "I know I don't have children of my own, a choice I made many years ago, but that doesn't mean I don't have human feelings."

Tola wondered where the conversation was headed. She also found it weird that Morieba, a stranger to all intents and purposes, would be the first woman she would be sitting that close to, for the first time in a long while, and her skin wasn't crawling.

"Let me just get straight to the point."

Morieba patted her hands, which were folded primly on her lap.

"You're the first person I'll be telling this, but I've found Alhaja's Will." She grinned. "Not only was I made the Sole Executor, I'm also Moremi's guardian."

The last sentence ricocheted around Tola's brain like a bullet.

"Please, not Moremi." She gripped Morieba's hand and made to kneel down. "Please don't take her away from me."

Tola heard the desperation in her own voice, the neediness that forced her to say those words. But she didn't care, she was beyond

caring. Moremi was her secret keeper.
Morieba lifted her up and Tola looked into her eyes. She took off her mask, she wanted Morieba to see, and maybe understand.
"I have no intention of 'taking Moremi away' from you as you put it." Morieba was implacable.
"Moremi is not a thing to be given or taken."
Tola recoiled at the accusation in her voice. Once again, the shame of the past, mixed with the long unacknowledged guilt of the present washed over her.
Morieba had been their housemaid, more of a chattel, a slave, she'd hated the way her parents treated her. And here she was an adult that should know better, enslaving a girl for close to five years. For the first time, the saying about apples not falling far from the tree made absolute sense to her.
I'm a hypocrite, just like everybody I'd ever judged, a bloody hypocrite!
"More importantly," Morieba's voice was gentle again, "Moremi is no longer a child, she will soon leave whether you like it or not."
Tola swallowed the truth of those words, bile in her throat.
"Here's what we are going to do," She said as Tola turned eyes brimming with tears towards her. "You, the children, Moremi and Kudirat will come and spend part of the holidays with me. By the time you return home, I would have found you a proper housekeeper, someone who will take good care of both you and the children. I will pay you and her a salary.."
A lifeline had just been thrown to her, she hadn't asked for it, but here it was, a chance to get away from Wale, to get her children away from him. Tola burst into tears.

season four
the wind,
the damn'd whirlwind
(2011-2012)

a whirlwind carried off the benenoise king

Kudirat clicked-clicked on killer high-heels towards the hall where the party was taking place. She walked dreamily, her short gown did what it was supposed to do, the exact way it had happened in her dreams, it floated on a cloud of chiffon. Dreams she had kept for so long in a secret compartment in her heart. A secret so dear to her she daren't share it in case the evils of the world, those who performed terrible deeds in the dead of the night, snatched her dreams away and killed it with their stabbing knives.

She felt lush, she was lush.

Her D-cup breasts that she had kept hidden away from eyes that would lust after them. Eyes that would judge her as loose just because of the way nature had made her. Breasts that had been locked underneath several layers of clothes since she'd started growing them were placed on display, to jiggle and wiggle. She pushed out her chest a little.

Her buttocks that had shamed her anytime she boarded a bus or a taxi and people started shouting about tiny girls with fat buttocks were shaken. Her rounded stomach that she'd wanted to exchange for Moremi's iron-board, flat stomach was not sucked in.

She was lush. She felt lush.

Her hair was combed out, the way she'd always wanted it. Thick, dark, bushy hair, softened with shea butter. She wore it - a crown. A touch of colour on her lids, purple, her lids were shadowed purple, her eyes lined with kohl, her lips coated black.

lakiriboto chronicles

Moremi had not wanted anybody mucking around with her face. "No make-up please, not even a light touch, thank you." The make-up artist that Morieba had employed to prepare them for the party had left in a huff.
Even at the tailor's Moremi had insisted that she didn't want to make a gown, she was never wearing another gown again.
Gowns symbolized sadness. They reminded her of the black, shapeless one she had to wear during Alhaja's burial, of the washed out ragged gowns she wore at Tola's house.
No more gowns!
So they made her a pair of trousers and a loose shirt.
Kudirat didn't have any problems with the gown that was made for her, in ankara and chiffon. Morieba's tailor was a genius. The gown was floaty, it stopped mid-thigh, the upper bodice was round necked, showing the tops of her generous cleavage, the sleeves were long and tight. Kudirat was wearing magic.
It had to be magic.
Barely three weeks ago she'd been a housemaid, stealing money, selling contraceptives. Running after snotty nosed kids, waking up at 4a.m. to clean and wash and prepare for school, a week ago she had been a slave.
But Oya, the all-seeing, all knowing whirlwind, had seen all that and had spoken to the cold, harsh wind that had been her life for the past five years, Oya had ordered the storms to cease and had given her warm, comforting breeze. She had decided to place her on a loving lap, the lap of luxury.
Kudirat was not one to go examining the teeth of a gift-horse. She would seize the moment, make use of every advantage thrown her way, she would be smart.
She was her mother's daughter.
The people of Alagbado had called her mother a whore, a husband snatcher, but her mother had seen a chance to leave the poverty of her life behind, and had seized it.
Her mother wasn't a husband snatcher, she was an opportunity snatcher.

She'd left the decrepit old farmer she'd been married to for a younger man searching for a son.

Although she hadn't seen the woman in over five years, the edicts her mother had passed down to her were her daily motto - be kind but do not allow anybody to make a fool out of you. Work hard, but better still, work smart. Take advantage of any opportunity that comes your way, but don't be greedy. Nothing lasts forever.

I am my mother's daughter.

She had taken the news that she and Moremi would be leaving Lagos for Aunty Morieba's house with a shrug. It was life and didn't it have a way of throwing surprises your way?

She had been somewhat bemused by the speed at which Tola had asked them to pack their things, and even more surprised at her energy. It was as if somebody had injected new life into Tola.

By the third day their things were ready.

"I'll be spending a week in Ibadan," Tola had said in reply to their surprised look when she'd fetched her suitcase out of her room too.

Three weeks later, Tola and her children were still at Morieba's. It appeared they had moved permanently into the little flat on the ground floor.

Morieba had made them dump everything they'd brought from Lagos and had taken them shopping.

Kudirat and Moremi had been hesitant, when they saw the price tags. The clothes were more expensive than all the money they'd been able to put together in all their years of stealing.

Morieba had started picking clothes and forcing it on them, when the girls realized she was not going to stop, they had gone to choose the things they wanted for themselves.

Kudirat, being of a practical turn of mind, decided to take everything happening to her as a dream, so she acted the way she would have in her dreams, a queen.

She stayed in bed and ordered breakfast from the cook, she ignored the children's screams, she watched TV, in the afternoon! She wore brand new clothes and new underwear, everyday! She sat in a car and was driven everywhere.

The closest she'd come to doing any household chores was putting her clothes in the washing machine and picking them up later, well ironed and neatly folded.
She was living the dream and for as long as it lasted, she would.
Within the week they had arrived Morieba had gone to register them in a school. A private school, with well-laid out, airy classes. Buildings that looked well-planned, beautifully painted classrooms, they had to drag her away from the science laboratory.
Kudirat's fingers were perpetually crossed, her breath in a state of suspension, she was afraid that if she breathed in too deeply she might wake up from this dream.
She crossed them again as they arrived on the red carpet. They were about to walk past the cameramen and photographers when Kudirat stopped.
"What is it now?" Moremi sounded exasperated.
"It's the Red Carpet, we have to wait for our photographs to be taken and then we'll get interviewed," Kudirat's eyes were huge.
She'd seen this done on TV before and had always wondered how it would feel standing in front of a camera. She flashed her most charming smile at the interviewer, a young man spotting a beard and a yellow bow tie. She pointed at Moremi who was rolling her eyes at her antics, "We are the celebrant's daughters."
The interviewer's eyes lit up as he scrutinized the girls, "We have a pair of angels on our hand." he murmured to the cameraman, who asked them to stand in front of a giant portrait of Morieba with 'Happy Birthday Pappy' splashed across it in bright red.
"I don't want to do this!" Moremi whispered to Kudirat.
"But you will do this, for me." Kudirat tugged at her arm, ignoring her deep frown.
The girls stood in front of the camera, Moremi scowling at her sneakers while Kudirat chatted, and laughed, and flirted with the camera.
"Pinch me quickly," Kudirat whispered as they got to the top of the staircase that led into the main body of the hall where the party was being held.
"Uh?"

"I said pinch me, so I'll know this is not a dream."
Moremi's squeezed up face relaxed into a smile. "Of course it has to be a dream, stuff like this doesn't happen in real life."
Kudirat moved closer to Moremi, suddenly nervous, "Do I look alright?"
Moremi took a long look at her, and Kudirat could see how beautiful she was in her eyes. "I shouldn't even be asking you, you're prejudiced."
"...and you are gorgeous," Moremi was still staring, making heat rush up on Kudirat's face. "If this is a dream, I don't want to wake up from it because of you. I've never seen you so happy before, and I want you to be happy."
Kudirat felt tears burn her lids but she pushed it back.
"You're just mean, you want to spoil my make-up because you are not wearing any."
They finally descended the staircase, Kudirat gripping Moremi's arms so she wouldn't fall off her high heeled shoes. As soon as she stepped off the last stair, she turned towards Moremi and yelled, "I want to dance."
"But shouldn't we find a table first?"
"Not if this is a dream, I don't want Oya or whoever is in charge, to wave her wand and make it all disappear before I dance in front of a life band led by Alhaji Igi-Sekele."
"What in the world are you on about?"
"You won't understand." Kudirat murmured.
Ngozi would, they both shared a love for Fújì music and filled their phones with songs from different fújì musicians.
Kudirat had grown up on Àpàlà and Fújì, which her father played early in the mornings and in the evenings, whenever there was power supply. The beats of wéré and talking drums comforted her, took her back to her days of innocence when her biggest worries had been whose compound she and her friends would steal mangoes from.
She suddenly missed Ngozi and the rest of the gang. She wanted to share her good fortune with them, show them what real happiness meant.

She would show them the washing machines, and hoovers, and all sorts of appliances that made the jobs they spent their days slaving over so easy. She would tell them that there were people trained to do all those jobs they did, made a good living from it and got days off. She wanted to tell them about being a teenager and being free from toil.

Moremi protested all the way to the stage where the musician was singing about a Beninoise King who was carried off by a whirlwind, to the frenetic beat of the snare drums.

Ewo ji toja togb' Oba aganyin
Ogbe Kofi, Nene,
I don't know,
I don't care...

Kudirat threw herself into the beat. It had been too long since she danced, too long since she let herself go and allowed the music to dictate the movement of her body.

Women in colourful Ankara and lace materials, made into different styles joined them on the dance floor. They carried their gèlè, twisted into mind bending designs, on elegantly held heads. They gyrated and twisted their waists to the music.

Not long afterwards men in long flowing agbádá joined them and started pasting their foreheads with brand new naira notes. The women were provoked into frenzied dance steps, hips were swaying, bosoms shaking while their gèlè gleefully defied the law of gravity.

Kudirat and Moremi climbed up the stage and started 'spraying' the musician with freshly minted hundred naira notes, given to them earlier by Morieba.

Kudirat was happy she had been able to convince Moremi to let them keep some of the money underneath their mattress before coming to the party. She knew if she had more she would have sprayed it all.

The band segued into another song and praised them to the high heavens. Nothing less than new dollar notes would do for him at that point.

Owo tuntun l'emi nfe
Kudirat o je naira,

O je Euro,
Oje pounds,
Otun je dollars repete

Not to be outdone, a gentleman, who looked dangerously close to delivering a set of triplets, joined them on stage and started throwing hundred dollar notes at them. Kudirat and Moremi stepped away from the melee as people scrambled madly for the money and tucked them into the pockets and bras.
"Kai but you girls are slow o! See how you were looking on like Lukman while those women grabbed the money that the man was spraying at you." Somebody said by their shoulder.
It was Tolu. Kudirat was her stepsister for the second time in her entire life.
Tolu was the daughter of the woman her mother had snatched her father from. She remembered Tolu's mother as Aunty L'Egba, the troublemaker that usually came to bug her dad about school fees.
She had met the young lady earlier in the week, in company of her mother, who was handling the catering for the party. L'Egba had simply pointed at her and said, 'that's your sister her name is Kudirat'. Tolu had shrugged and walked away, it surprised her that she was suddenly being friendly.
"You guys look alike." Moremi said softly.
The similarity in the line of their jaws and dainty noses, even their height and blue-black skin hue, was so much they could easily pass for twins.
"We should, after all we share the same father." Tolu said dismissively.
Kudirat looked away in embarrassment. Nobody talked about stuff like that, there was too much history. Too many people had been hurt by decisions taken by the adults in their lives.
She felt that Tolu resented her, but she shouldn't have bothered wasting her emotions. After all their dad hadn't practically sold her into slavery.
An uncomfortable silence descended on the trio as they dragged

chairs around an empty table. Kudirat's stomach reminded her that she had barely eaten all day, so she waved frantically at one of the servers bearing a tray full of plates of food, but was ignored.
"What's this nonsense? I'm hungry!" She protested as another tray was carried past their table.
"You girls are truly learners. You'd better go to one of the serving points and order what you want or you're going to be ignored all night." Tolu said.
Of course we are learners, we've spent the past five years cooped up with a perv and his mad wife! Sprang to Kudirat's lips but she swallowed the words, she was ashamed of calling Tola mad, even in her mind.
Kudirat jumped out of the chair and tottered towards one of the several serving points scattered around the tent.
"Helluur," She used the fakest Lagos accent she could summon, "My muom," She swept the room a look and spotted Morieba at a table filled with fat, yellow women and all kinds of alcohol. She waved at her, "Said I should cuom and tawk to you, that you'll take gewd currof uz."
The young man nodded and before long, Kudirat was leading, triumphantly, a train of servers bearing different kinds of food and drinks. The servers laid out the table while Kudirat returned to the drinks stand. She was back a few minutes later grinning like the cat that got the cream.
"Okay, tell me what you've done." Moremi said after a short staring contest between her and the smirking Kudirat.
Kudirat pulled her arm from underneath the table and flourished a bottle of Irish Cream under Moremi's nose.
"We are fulfilling another fantasy tonight."
"I'm not drinking that!" Moremi protested.
"Oh yes you are!" Kudirat poured generous shots into three glasses. "Remember the night you convinced me not to drink too much of the one on Dr Wale's liquor shelf..." She trailed off as she remembered him, she wondered again, as she'd been wondering since they arrived in Ibadan, if he knew where his wife was.
"I remember no such thing!" Moremi protested before she'd even

completed her sentence. Kudirat had lost the heart to hound Moremi so she fell quiet.

She shivered with trepidation at what could happen if Dr Wale didn't know his wife was in Ibadan. Kudirat dropped the bottle on the table and sighed mournfully.

"I suggest you hide that bottle because here comes Anti Morieba." Tolu said her eyes fixed on her phone.

The girls turned guiltily, but instead of Morieba, they found Quadri-the-bookworm standing behind them.

Quadri was another person they'd met at Aunty Morieba's house. He was one of Olori Ebi's sons. Kudirat had decided she didn't like him because Moremi said the son of a snake was a snake.

He flashed them a sharky smile.

"Am I not the luckiest man in the world? Finding a bevy of beauties sitting all by themselves, who are feeling lonesome and unappreciated, is a rare honour." He sat down and beamed at them.

"Stuff your cheesy words jo." Kudirat said contemptuously. "We are your cousins, you're not supposed to be looking at us like that and I don't remember anybody asking you to sit on that chair."

"Kudi baby, even though you're my second cousin, twice removed or something like that, I don't think it's fair that you'd deny me the pleasure of basking in the light of your beauty and eating part of this spread." He paused, "Tasting the Irish cream you're hiding underneath the table will also be nice."

"Are you for real?" Moremi frowned at him.

"Oh yes I am for real, my third cousin Moremi, whatever that means, and I can always call Anti Morieba to seek her opinion on this matter, since she's standing right over there." Quadri waved at Morieba, who smiled at him and waved back.

"Stop teasing the girls, Quadri." Tolu admonished him. "Don't mind Quadri, he might be one of Olori Ebi's sons but he's totally cool."

The girls relaxed and started heaping food on their plates. Within a short while most of the food on the table had disappeared and the bottle of Irish cream was nearly empty. They were all giggling and talking affectionately to one another.

lakiriboto chronicles

Quadri disappeared and after a while returned with a bottle of wine.
"Good boy Quadri." Kudirat said as he sat down.
"I haven't seen your dad tonight." Tolu said.
Moremi's expression froze.
"Oh he's not coming. He hates Anti Morieba too much to watch her being happy. She's the antithesis of everything he believes a woman should be. She's rich, young, unmarried and independent. She doesn't need him. To worsen things she has just snatched darling Moremi from underneath is nose, with all her gorgeous money." He said casually. "He told members of the family not to attend this party and placed curses on anybody who dared to."
Quadri looked around the tent and laughed, "I guess he's not as feared as he imagines himself to be, or the lure of Àríyá had been more powerful, or isn't that table filled with the Alagbado's both home and abroad?"
The three girls strained their necks towards the table Quadri was using his chin to point at, and truly, the table was filled with people they were familiar with, family members from Alagbado Village were even present.
Quadri shrugged, popped a fried meat in his mouth and continued talking as soon as he swallowed the meat. "He's just jealous, he wants all the money in the whole world to belong to him. He has control issues, he loves it when people are in awe of him or are dependent on him."
"Don't be silly, your dad is not that bad." Tolu said in a tone that implied she did not mean what she was saying. She had taken her gaze off her phone and was absorbing everything Quadri was saying through her pores.
"Oh yes he is. He's worse than you'd imagine, you obviously don't know him." He uncorked the wine.
"And you're being so casual about it?" Moremi was baffled. "Isn't he your father?"
Quadri lifted an eyebrow. "How else should I be? Go around scowling and being generally unhappy because my father is a mean bastard? I refuse to be like my brothers, who pretend to be like him so that he would love them. The only person my father loves is

himself." He smiled, "You people are young, so you won't understand."

"It's good that you're all happy about the way your dad goes about destroying people's lives, taking things that don't belong to him, but I don't think I'll ever forgive him for what he did to me," Moremi said hotly.

"Don't get all worked up, what he's done to you is mild stuff compared with what he's done to other people. I can tell you stuff about Baami that would make your toes curl. Do you know I met my mother for the first time this year? I'm nineteen years old and for most of my life I actually believed she was dead because Baami told me so." He picked a piece of chicken from one of the platters on the table and passed the bottle of wine to Tolu. The girls stared at him goggle eyed.

"What? Why are you all staring at me like that?" He said.

"You're talking about Olori Ebi," Kudirat whispered the name as if saying it any louder would summon the man into their presence.

"I used to believe everything he told me ... until I met my mum. I've discovered that the only way to make my father powerless against you is by being indifferent to him and his theatrics." His voice deepened into a whisper and he turned serious all of a sudden. "You plan your moves against him, quietly. You smile at him and pretend to obey his instructions and then go ahead to do what you want to, exactly how you want to."

"So are you going to move in with your mum?" Moremi asked after a heartbeat.

"No," He straightened up and took another sip of his wine. "He doesn't even know that my mother finally found me or that I know that she's alive. My mum is genuinely afraid of him, so, no, I will stay with him until I collect my admission letter and then I'm off. He's made it clear to us all that he's not going to pay our fees past secondary school anyway, and he has many sons, I don't think he'd be too worried about me."

He looked straight into Moremi's eyes. "By the way Moremi, I'd be careful. Baami doesn't give up easily and I know he's up to something," he leaned in and whispered, "Watch your back!"

lakiriboto chronicles

Èsù drew up a chair and sat beside Àríyá the god of great Yoruba parties, who was ensuring that the celebration was going on smoothly by sprinkling excitement and giddiness intermittently in the air.
"These Alagbado's really know how to throw it down! Abeg, pass me that Ciroc."

back to reality . . .

Tola walked around Agodi Gardens, marveling at how much things had changed. She felt as if she was seeing Ibadan for the first time. Everything her gaze fell upon had a patina of glitter.
She could truly see, she was looking around instead of constantly looking inside. The windows of her mind were thrown open, and she gloried in the sunshine.
Her sneakers clad feet danced down walkways. She gave them freedom to lead her where they would. And they remembered. Her feet remembered her favorite places, they led her to the little corner where she used to feed the monkeys, to a tree that she climbed as a child. Her feet knew her path to happiness.
Tola followed her feet.
The garden was one of the few places in Ibadan (or anywhere else for that matter), that held good memories for her.
Memories of Easters past, when as a child, her family would picnic in the garden. Because the church posters always announced the picnic as 'Going to Galilee to watch Jesus rise from the Grave', for a long time Tola believed Agodi was the town of Galilee.
It was the only place where she had been allowed to be a child. She and her sister, Kemi, would chase each other round the trees, playing hide and seek with other children, they would feed the animals and climb the trees.

As she grew older, she not only discovered that Agodi was not Galilee, she also found out that she didn't like being with the humans. So she started taking explorative walks into its heart, farther and farther away from her parents, the church, her sister. The same way she had been distancing herself from them in real life.

She would deliberately lose herself in the trees and flowers, in the chirping of birds, the howling of monkeys. Only returning to the group when it was nearly time to leave.

A monkey chattered at her from one of the trees that populated the nature conservatory, Tola chattered back at it and threw it the rest of her biscuits.

Lagos had become a distant memory, her brain had somehow managed to shut down that part of her life as if life with Wale had been a dream, an insubstantial nightmare.

Her phone jangled, she pulled it out of her pocket and checked the caller ID. It was Kudirat.

"Hello."

"Aunty, you'd better come home now, now, now!" Kudirat's panic reached through the phone and grabbed her by the throat.

"The children..."

"The children ke? Aunty, this one pass the children o! There is fire on the mountain! Your mummy and Uncle Wale are shouting."

The sound of scuffling filled Tola's ears as Kudirat's voice faded from the phone.

"Hello, Hello, Kudirat are you still there? Helloooo." she was about dropping the call when Moremi's calm voice came over the phone.

"Hello Aunty Tola, it's me Moremi."

"What's going on there?"

"I think you should come home, some people are looking for you."

"And they are shouting at Aunty Morieba," Kudirat yelled into the phone. More scuffling noises.

"Hello, Aunty Tola are you still there?" Moremi sounded a little out of breath.

"Yes, yes, I'm still here."

Even as Tola spoke those words her legs were already making their way towards the exit.

"Just come home."
As she waited for a taxi, Tola weighed her options. She could leave now and never look back. She could hide and wait them out, she could return to Agodi Gardens and take out her SIM card.

But that wasn't the way to treat a woman who had given her a chance, no questions asked, and Wale would have won, he would have the children. She died a little inside, it wasn't a thought she even wanted to contemplate.

More importantly, where would she go? Yes she had some money in her bank account, money that she'd siphoned from their joint account over the years, but what about headaches? What about Rita? In the past few months she had somehow managed to control Rita and her appetites.

She still had days when the whisper of feet on the floor would send her scurrying into the bedroom, doors locked, windows barred.

But it was somehow not as bad as it used to be, it was like an extra darkness had been lifted off the one in her.

Nobody ever comes to tell her to stop it or get out of bed.

She didn't know what miracle Morieba had performed but the children seemed to be more understanding. She could stay in her darkness and somehow feel safe. Morieba made it okay for her to stay in the darkness without the extra fear of someone coming to loom over her, an expression of disgust on his face.

She hailed a taxi.

As Tola alighted in front of Morieba's house, she braced herself for the onslaught of the high Italian opera she was about to participate in.

The gate was opened for her by Kudirat, Mr Sule, the gateman, hovered in the background.

"Grandma and Dr Wale and Olori Ebi are waiting for you." She said as Tola stepped into the compound. "The children are in your flat with Moremi," she lowered her voice, "we've told them to keep quiet or Ojuju-Calabar will carry them off."

Tola smiled faintly, not one but three Ojuju Calabar were already waiting to swoop them back into a dungeon. Her children's greatest enemies was not some mythical masquerade from Calabar, they were up close and personal.

"There she is!" Her mum shrieked from somewhere near the front door. She was suddenly surrounded by her mother, Olori Ebi and Wale.

"Where are the children?" they all asked in different tones, Wale's was soft, her mum's was a shriek, Olori Ebi's a resounding boom. Tola shut out their voices and walked towards the house.

She was pulled back roughly by Wale. "You are not taking another step until I see my children."

"Jesus my saviour, my Lord, who has done this to my child?" Tola's mother had taken off her scarf and wrapped it round her waist. "This is the handiwork of my enemies."

She shut her eyes and started praying. "Oh Lord of Esau, Lord of Jacob, Lord of Israel, bring fire down and consume all my enemies. All those who are jealous of my child's marital success shall die by fire. Bring down the mountains oh lord and they shall become like mud underneath my feet, let my enemies die, by fire, die! Die! Die!"

Tola expelled a breath of disgust and stepped away from her mother who had added jumping to her shrieking. She went on like that for close to five minutes, and everybody froze in reverence to the bile and hate gushing out of her in the form of prayers.

Èsù stepped closer to Iya Tola and studied the different expressions her face.

"If there's any witch or enemy here, it's you mother." Tola said when she couldn't take it any longer.

Her mother stopped mid-tirade, her mouth agape, she held her breasts in consternation.

It was an unspoken rule that nobody interrupts when she was praying. People were expected to stand in awe of her prowess, her use of words as a sword of righteousness, a sword of instant judgement.

"Iya Tola," Olori Ebi interjected, "I've told you that Morieba's juju is strong, we need to get your poor daughter and her children away from her before it's too late."

"I am not going anywhere." Tola muttered defiantly.

"What did you just say?" Olori Ebi growled.
"You are coming with us whether you like it or not." Wale was still in character as the hard-done-by, valiant man.
Tola looked at him fully in the face, "Is it so that you can have access to the children and do your evil with them?"
Wale looked at her with contempt. "I told you Olori Ebi, this girl is mad, can you imagine what she's saying?"
"You know what?" Olori Ebi lowered his tone until it became a soothing rumble. "I think we should all calm down." He turned towards Tola with something that might have been a smile. "We'll go to my place and discuss this. At the end of the day you can either decide to either stay here or return to Lagos with your husband."
Tola looked at each one of them. They had that determined look on their faces. They were ready to make trouble.
Maybe it's even better this way.
"Okay, let me go and inform Aunty Morieba that-"
She was dragged back by Wale, "You don't seem to understand what I'm saying. I want my children and you're not leaving this spot until I see them."
"Calm down Wale," Olori Ebi patted him on the back. "Legs are removed from a pair of trousers one after the other. We will sort everything out." He gave Tola that tic pretending to be a smile again. "You may go and tell her. We'll wait here for you, please don't take too long."
Tola felt triumphant as she left the rabble behind. She half expected Rita to congratulate her on winning that battle.
Morieba met her at the door. "So what have you decided?"
"We'll be going to Olori Ebi's house for a meeting." She took Morieba's hand in hers, "I'm sorry about the embarrassment."
Morieba patted the back of her hand. "It's alright Tola, if they'd been civil, I would have been surprised. You're an adult and should be allowed to make your own decisions."
"I have made up my mind Morieba, I'm not returning to Lagos, they can't make me."
She snorted in disgust. "Just take care of yourself and watch your back. That old man can't be trusted."

season four: the wind, the damn'd whirlwind (2011-2012)

"I understand," Tola pulled open the door, "I'll see you later."
She stepped out of the hallway and pulled the door shut. She closed her eyes and leaned her head against the door, a dull throbbing had started behind her eyelids, she pushed it away.
She was ill prepared, she didn't have any plans, she'd naively assumed she could hide out in Morieba's house forever.
After a few more minutes of taking deep breaths, she straightened away from the door and went to join the wandering troubadours.
"I'll sit in front with Wale, you sit at the back with your mother." Olori Ebi ordered as they got to the car.
The drive to Olori Ebi's house, in the heart of Idi-Ikan, would have been dead quiet if Iya Tola hadn't been muttering prayers.
"I am not returning to Lagos with Wale," Tola said as soon as they all settled down in Olori Ebi's sitting room, "As far as I'm concerned our marriage is over."
Tola's mother jumped out of her seat. "That will not be your portion in Jesus name! My daughter will not be a single parent or a divorcee! I serve a living God, and he shall not allow my feet to be moved, the God of Israel does not sleep nor slumber, a thousand shall fall..."
"Ah, that's enough!" Olori Ebi hissed impatiently.
Wale watched all of them with an air of disinterest.
"So, Tola, what led to this decision?"
Tola thought about the question, she knew the answers. She didn't love Wale, she'd never loved him. She had married him because her parents told her to. But those kind of sentiments wouldn't hold water with these two, they don't hold truck with love and all that rubbish.
Should she tell them about Jesutofunmi, but what evidence does she have? The meds?
Why do I need to justify myself? Why can't they just accept my decision?
"He's been giving me medications without my knowledge." She blurted out.
"Ngbó Wale?" Olori Ebi turned towards him.
"I don't know why we are holding this meeting when you all know quite well that your daughter is mental!" Wale's air of disinterest had hardened into cold rage.

"How can a woman leave her marital home, with her children, without informing anybody? She just disappeared. I've nearly gone mad searching for her all over Lagos. It wasn't until yesterday that her mother called that I found out she'd been in Ibadan all along." He narrowed his eyes at Iya Tola. "I am not even sure this was not a plan between mother and daughter!"

Iya Tola was out of the chair in a flash, "Wale how can you say such a thing?"

"Sit down woman!" Olori Ebi barked, "continue what you were saying my dia son-in-law."

The moment Olori Ebi said those words Tola's heart sank. She knew the outcome of the meeting.

She tightened her face.

I won't let them bully me.

Wale pointed a dramatic, shaky finger at her. "This woman is an ingrate! She had not only accused me of molesting my own daughter, she'd also threatened to kill me. In fact she can stay in Ibadan for all I care! I just want my children back."

Tola cringed as her mother knelt in front of Wale. "Don't be like that my son-in-law, please don't let her foolishness separate you."

"Mama please stand up." Wale pulled her mother up.

Tola wanted to tear up her hair, she wanted to throw herself on the ground and weep. Her mother pleading with Wale was a taste of the humiliation she knew was in store for her, she suddenly realized the extent of her powerlessness.

The oasis that living with Morieba for a few weeks had been, was a mirage. Her paranoia kicked in, she knew without a shadow of doubt that she was in thrall of powers that were way beyond her.

I'm so fucked.

"As I was saying Olori Ebi," Wale was in charge. He flashed her a triumphant look. "We all know about Tola's condition. I knew about it before I married her. I thought I could manage her condition," he turned towards Iya Tola, "Am I lying?"

Iya Tola shook her head mutely, her head downcast.

You married me off at 17 because you couldn't bear me.

Tola swallowed those words.

Of course they thought they were doing it for her. After taking her to several churches, even her mother had eventually consented to her seeing herbalists, but nothing had worked.

A memory peeped through, of being tied down, a live cock rubbed over her naked body by an old man with rotten teeth... she tucked it in.

Olori Ebi sighed loudly. "It is one's yam that causes the fingers to be dipped in palm-oil. It is quite entertaining watching a mad man dance naked in the market place," He gave Tola a meaningful stare, "but a mad man is not a thing to be desired as a child. Wale, please go on."

"I took her to see a psychiatrist after she had our last child and fell into deep depression."

Tola looked at Wale wide eyed, that was the first time she'd be hearing that she'd been to see a psychiatrist. Or was he telling the truth?

"I even took her to see a female psychiatrist! One of my colleagues, Dr Adejana," Wale continued, "She was the one that recommended the meds to her, these are just ordinary multi-vitamins and anti-depressants. We started out with benzodiazepines, but when that one was not working, she said that we should put her on a course of Zyprexa or Seroquel."

Olori Ebi cleared his throat, "Ekùn! That's my Doctor! See how he's speaking big-big grammar."

Tola's head began to pound in earnest, she stepped aside for Rita.

"In the past six months, it appeared that the medicine was actually working! I had hopes that things would turn around, but I was wrong!" Wale shifted his attention from his enraptured audience and turned to face her. "Here's the thing, I will not force you to return to Lagos with me. However, I'm taking my children, because I cannot allow them to be raised by a psychotic woman."

"My in-law you don't have to say anything further." Olori Ebi faced the woman he presumed to be Tola.

"I think you've heard all the things your husband has said, and as your father's best friend, your father and also the head of this family, I order you to return to your husband's house!" Olori Ebi's voice rose

in volume, he moved to the edge of his seat. "Do not allow a jealous woman who has neither husband nor children ruin your marriage. A woman without a husband is like a king without his crown. Do not allow someone use jazz to spoil your head."
Rita studied him closely, the frantic manner his Adam's apple ran up and down his neck, his dark, thick lips, his surprisingly white teeth, those plump cheeks, his pink tongue dotted black in patches... she giggled.
"I'm so fucked."
Iya Tola burst into tears and started praying, "All you spirit of wickedness, the spirit of madness that wish to take over my daughter, I bind you in Jesus' name! I bid you depart!"
"I told you Olori Ebi she's mad!" Wale jumped out of his seat, "In fact I'm leaving, I will go and pick my children."
Rita kept laughing, she laughed so hard tears were streaming down her face. She was laughing at herself, at the corner in which she'd been boxed. She laughed at them, because they had no idea...
"I don't know what that woman has told you to make you think you can leave with my children!" Wale blazed at her, ignoring Iya Tola who was clinging to his leg, tears running down her cheeks, mouth filled with words of self-abasement. She was promising him heaven and earth, if only...please my husband, please don't chase her away...
"I will take those children from you!" He was on a roll, "You will never see them again!"
Olori Ebi who had been staring at her with barely concealed dismay shouted, "Enough of all these Tola, What is funny about us? You think we're here to play?" He rose from his seat and loomed over the tableau. "I have heard that you're mad, but now I can see how very mad you really are."
The hysteria in the room rose a notch as Wale turned towards Olori Ebi, "I already warned you sir, this is what I live with on a daily basis and I'm done!"
Tola's head pounded harder as the noise level increased with everyone shouting at her. Butressing one another's points, emphasizing how mad she was.

Mad woman...Crazy girl... Medicine... Seroquel... Delusional...
Rita burst into tears, shocking them all into silence.
"This matter has passed 'be careful' o," Olori Ebi looked at her warily, "I hope she won't start tearing her clothes off now."
"She's actually not violent," Wale said in the tones of The-One-Who-Knows, "I think it's because she's not been taking her medicine."
Olori Ebi looked at him in admiration. "Ah well done Wale, so you've been managing this madness all these years without complaining?"
"I'll return to Lagos with you," Rita muttered, she straightened her spine, wiped her face and looked at them soberly, "I'll return to Lagos with you."
"Praise God!" Iya Tola shouted.

photographs in sepia

Moremi envied Kudirat. She envied the easy way she had settled into their new life, taking the ups as easily as she had taken the downs. She envied her laid back, shit happens and we are all going to die someday attitude.
She acknowledged her flaw, that huge thing which sometimes kept her awake at night – intensity. How she felt everything, how she bottled up everything.
And everything included — her fears about her mother. An abiding, hour on the hour thing - that her mother was dead, that she'd overdosed on heroin and was now a vegetable, rotting away in some dank corner of Nigeria. Or worse still, that she was one of the teeming masses of junkies that littered the streets — begging, stealing, prostituting. That one day, she'd run into her and her mother wouldn't recognize her.
She bottled up those moments when she missed her grandmother, so painfully that her chest would contract, her lungs gasping for air.
Inside that bottle was also her deep seated hatred for Olori Ebi and Wale. Her resentment of Tola, who had burdened her with more secrets - as if she did not have enough of her own.

lakiriboto chronicles

She hadn't even known how to name all these emotions until she'd met Miss Akunne, the counsellor in her new school. The feelings just roiled and bubbled inside of her and sometimes the pressure would build up in her head until it was fit to burst.
It was during those moments that she lashed out, at the nearest object, or person, who was usually Kudirat, her whipping boy.
When they had resumed in their new school she had been so sullen and uncommunicative in class that she'd been sent in to see Miss Akunne.
She had been going in to see the counsellor regularly, for fifteen minutes every day.
The woman had given her books to read, and new words to express how she felt.
Miss Akunne would listen, for fifteen minutes, whether she spoke or not and gradually, Moremi talked, about her grandmother, her mother, about Tola and years of servitude.
Her sessions with the school counsellor only served to add to the list of things she worried about, because the school was a far cry from Bariga High School.
The school itself was built in form of a square around a vast field, where students played games in the afternoon.
There were different buildings and classes for different subjects. The teachers were polite and well-educated, they even seem to enjoy teaching.
Instead of blackboards, there were white-boards connected to the internet. iPads had replaced text and notebooks.
Instead of getting caned they were sent in to see Miss Akunne or other counsellors that worked with her.
Their science laboratories were actual laboratories, not the empty, dirty hall, with rusted pipes, broken pipettes and empty bottles with faded handwritten titles on them.
Where Bariga Comprehensive High School was a collection of buildings made out of broken dreams and desperate hopes. Berger High School was the actualization of dreams, where you were spoon-fed knowledge, according to your taste.

The students were friendly and easy going. They spoke a language that was so advanced Moremi sometimes wondered if she was still in a secondary school or a university. Words like intersectionality, politics of colour and race, radicalism, feminism were casually thrown around.
On Fridays the school was dressed in a wild array of colours. They dropped the names of designers she'd only watched on E! as casually as they dropped their surnames in the most harmless of conversations.
They all loved Kudirat because she was so 'quaint' and 'traditional'. She lapped it all up, and hammed it anytime they were at the cafeteria, holding conversations. She would drop her aitches, indiscriminately, like soft boiled eggs.
They thought Moremi was 'lucky' to have lived an 'authentic African lifestyle', her Yoruba was so 'effortless'.
"Wow! You so have to teach me how to speak Yoruba properly."
Moremi missed Bariga High School, with its uncomplicated students and a system stripped of pretenses.
Bariga High was a jungle, only the most cunning survived. At Berger High, name dropping was an art form.
They wanted to know the meaning of her name, "Were you named after that Ife Princess/warrior/spy? Or does the name have other meanings?"
They wanted her to talk to them about being bi-racial, they held group discussions about being part Russian/Eriterian/Igbo, we are all mixed you know.
They threw wild parties on weekends where everybody got high on illegal substances, including love. Parties that Moremi attended for two reasons: to watch Kudirat dance and to kiss girls in dark corners.
"I love, love your aunt," a girl called Trixie had sighed one morning as they walked through the school reception area together, "In fact I think I have a little crush on her, she's so butch."
She skittered away after getting one of Moremi's blank faced stares.
Everything about the school whispered in sophistication, air-kisses, international travel and centuries of wealth ... at least that was the

impression Moremi got.

It had started insidiously enough, her new fear, but the longer she stayed with Morieba and realised that she might never have to struggle against poverty again, it grew bigger.

She worried about the amount of money Morieba was spending to keep them in the school, the amount she spent on the new clothes she kept buying for them, clothes with designer labels not knock-downs or rip-offs. She even worried about the amount of food she and Kudirat were eating.

On the days that her anxieties weren't so bad, she suspected Morieba was doing all those things more for herself than them. The seriousness with which she'd taken up her role as an adoptive mother to two teenage girls spoke of careful planning, years of secret yearnings.

"I've been reading up about teenagers, and according to the book, this is when you're at your most vulnerable. We need to work on your self-esteem."

It had all been fun and games when they had first arrived in Ibadan, a dream so good you didn't want to wake up from it. She had enjoyed her Cinderella experience with the same childish gleefulness that Kudirat did, it wasn't until they'd walked down the corridors of Berger High School to be registered that it dawned on her that life had really changed, that she'd never have to be a housemaid again. Her fortunes had finally changed.

But it wasn't hers, the fortune, it belonged to Morieba, and Moremi worried that at the rate they were going they would soon deplete her resources and Morieba would come to resent them.

She did not want that to happen and this gave her the impetus to walk down the long corridor to Morieba's room. She knocked on the door before her fears made her walk away.

Miss Akunne had insisted that fears were to be faced, she'd asked her the worst that could happen.

"Come in."

She pushed open the door and stepped into the room on quiet feet.

"Good morning Moremi," her ever cheerful aunt smiled at her, she was in bed with the curtains drawn, the air was crispy and scented with the expensive perfumes Morieba wore.

"Shut the door after you and come and lie beside me."

"Good morning Aunty," Moremi climbed into bed with her aunt. She pulled the covers over herself and snuggled into Morieba.

"I love having you here with me." She pulled Moremi closer. Morieba was always saying things like that, she called it positivity, speaking love.

"I've come to discuss something with you," Moremi said hesitantly, not because she was afraid of Morieba, but she didn't know how to start. "I'm worried about school."

Morieba froze, "Have they been bullying you? Are you having academic problems?"

"No, no aunty," Moremi laughed at her fierceness, she had no doubt that her aunt would deal with anyone that dared bully her. "I'm worried about the school fees."

"Bah! How much is it that you're worrying?"

"You're paying in dollars aunty, the money runs into millions of naira! And that's not counting all the clothes, and the shoes and the feeding."

"I can afford it." Morieba said dismissively. "I grew up in extreme poverty. Before the age of ten I learnt how to take care of myself. I lost both parents before I turned five, and I'm sure you've heard the story of how I was passed around like a battered luggage before your grandmother finally took me in. I worked for this money, I, Morieba Alagbado," she pounded her chest. "I know the name of wealth and I use it. My wealth is not dependent on the vagaries of the Nigerian economy. Are you familiar with the Yoruba word, àgbàná?"

Moremi shook her head.

"Àgbàná is the spirit of wastefulness, according to legend, when this spirit possesses your money, you end up destitute, but I'm so rich that if àgbàná enters my money through one end, it would emerge from the other end confused. I can live anywhere in the world and still remain a very wealthy woman. I'm far from poor, so you have nothing to worry about."

Moremi decided to take another track. "Do you know how much my

grandmother left to me?"
Morieba paused fetched her phone from the table and started rifling through it, "I'm not so sure," she picked a pair of reading glasses off the bedside table and placed it on her nose. "Ah, here's the list. She left about forty million naira, in her various accounts. She has four houses at Bodija and one shopping mall at Gate. She has two other houses somewhere in Ikoyi and another one in Lekki."
All the facts and figures Morieba was throwing around didn't mean much to Moremi, but it was reassuring, so she forged ahead.
"Do you think Olori Ebi has spent all the money?"
"I know he has been collecting the rents on the houses and shopping mall," a faint smile crossed her face, "but he doesn't have access to the money in the banks. They have strict rules about relatives and papers and such like that."
"Here's the thing aunty."
Moremi was impressed by Morieba's openness, she doubted that adults discussed their financial status with 17 year old girls.
"Do you have access to the papers to the house and accounts?"
The question gave Morieba another pause, "Actually, I've been so preoccupied with finding the Will that I hadn't even thought about the title deeds, but I think I know where all those things are stored."
"I want us to find all those papers aunty, I want you to use my grandmother's money to send Kudirat and I to school. And invest the rest for us. That way you're helping me to secure my future and at least I will stop worrying about burdening you with our school fees. Kudirat and I have discussed this, and we've decided that we should spend an extra year in school, maybe take one of their advanced classes while we sit for JAMB or apply to one of those medical schools abroad."
"Your head is correct!" Moremi gave her a hug, "Your head is correct like the thrift collector of Somolu."
Moremi lifted her head off the pillow and looked straight into her aunt's eyes, "My head is not correct Aunty Morieba, I have just decided I will no longer be a victim, no longer a pawn to be pushed around by people. I am taking control of my money, of my life and

that's how it should be!"

Morieba touched her cheek tenderly, "You're now an adult."

They made arrangements to go to her grandmother's house at Idi-Ikan on Saturday morning.

Moremi planned the outfit she would be wearing with meticulous care. She chose and discarded so many clothes that Kudirat started teasing her about how vain she was acting, 'or is there someone at Idi-Ikan you're hoping to impress?'

"I don't want anybody to recognize me," Moremi tried to make her understand. "You see all those people, they know me. They've known me from my childhood. Those children that we all played together when I was growing up, would be there, staring at me."

"Why is that so important? Isn't it their eyes? They can use it to do anything they like." Kudirat retorted.

"The staring in Lagos, that one I can even take. Those ones are looking at me as if I'm a white person, but these ones, they know me as Moremi."

Kudirat scrunched up her face, the book she'd been reading dangling off her fingers.

"They know," Moremi groaned.

"What do they know?"

"Look here," Moremi shut her wardrobe and sat beside Kudirat on the cold marble floor. "See when I was growing up, I was the richest girl in our neighbourhood. I had all the latest toys, I even had a bicycle, but now instead of returning from abroad or school or something very important, I'm returning as the girl who used to be a housemaid." Moremi hung her head as shame flooded her face pink. "They'll all be laughing at me. And you know how I hate being laughed at."

She had finally settled on a pair of baggy jeans, an oversized t-shirt with a hoodie and a pair of timberlands. She was quietly nervous throughout the drive to Idi-Ikan. But she shouldn't have worried, the neighbourhood was deserted, except for a few naked children playing hopscotch in front of the house across from her grandmother's.

As they alighted from the car, they were met by Iya Ruka, who gave a scream and hugged Moremi.

"Moremi my Moremi," She hugged her again, and pushed her hoodie off. "See how tall you have grown, even taller than me." She turned Moremi around. "What have they been feeding you in that your Lagos? Hee God I thank you o! So I will still see you on this side of heaven?"

After fussing over Moremi for a few more minutes she fetched the key to the house from a cloth bag tied around her waist, underneath her wrapper and opened the gate.

Moremi held herself stiffly, afraid she might shatter if she allowed herself to absorb how decrepit her childhood home had become. The front yard had been over-taken by weeds, she didn't want to imagine what the backyard looked like. As for the main house itself, it looked like an old man that had given up on life. Peeling paint, dark patches. The wooden windows that used to be thrown open to let in light and air were tightly shut.

"Sorry about the way grass is just growing anyhow," Iya Ruka interjected into the silence, "we are only cutting it once in a year, when we want be do party, abi when we want be do meeting."

Moremi swallowed a smile, at least that one thing had not changed, Iya Ruka's habit of speaking English.

"We need to do something about this Iya Ruka." Morieba said. "This house was meant to be lived in, not deserted like a graveyard."

"Ah, last year I axe Olori Ebi to let me be coming to be live here and be take care of everytin. My husband he yaff marry new wife, and she is a trouble woman. But Olori Ebi didn't gree. He pain me well-well." Iya Ruka unlocked the main door and pushed it open.

"Thank you Iya Ruka, we'll take it from here," Morieba reached out for the keys. The woman hesitated, and cleared her throat. "Don't worry," Morieba smiled at her, "I brought something for you, I'll give it to you before we leave."

The woman returned the smile and dipped her knees before dropping the keys on Morieba's open palm.

Morieba fidgeted with the light switch by the door, the musty smell of a house dying from neglect clogged Moremi's throat, alongside memories.

She was mentally reliving the first time she'd stepped into the house, hesitatingly, just as she was doing now. An intense 5year old who didn't say much. Her first real birthday party thrown lavishly for her, the cakes, the candles, the party games. Finally learning how to smile, laughing as her grandmother tickled her.

She stepped into the big parlour, the pictures were still there. Sepia coloured photos of ancestors past, frowning down at her through fogged over glass, from their lofty position in the skies above.

She closed that memory and pulled open another one, the smaller parlour, where she'd spent evenings on her grandmother's lap, having her hair matted, reading, or being read to. Nights of watching Yoruba Nollywood films that her grandmother had been so fond of, on the old colour TV and CD.

The cabinet that used to house those gadgets gaped emptily at her, one of its wooden frames hung forlornly, giving the whole cabinet a lopsided look.

Her mother's face, when she had been young and pretty and happy. Moremi took a closer look at the pictures on the walls, of her mother's growing up years. She noted, for the first time, how her mother's face had changed, from that of a happily smiling child, to the last one.

Her mother must have been 18 or so when the photograph had been taken. She was seated on a long stool, her back turned to the camera, she was looking over her shoulder, was that desperation in her eyes, pain? Moremi stood on tiptoes and fetched the picture off the wall, and then another, and then another, until she had them all off.

She was still studying the pictures, trying to track when that desperation had crept into her mother's eyes when Morieba touched her, bringing her back into the present.

"We will return another day. The house will be cleaned and repainted. Let's go and find what we came here for."

Without a backward glance at the picture frames she had piled on the table, Moremi followed her aunt to her grandmother's room.

Like every other part of the house, thick dust had settled on every available surface, the room smelt damp, making Moremi's nostrils itch.

"She kept the papers in a box underneath her bed. In fact I should have thought of that first," Morieba said as she knelt on the floor, unheeding of getting her clothes dirty. "She had a copy of the Will in that box too. She had everything organised and we were supposed to take it for safekeeping at her bank."

Moremi joined her on the floor as she started pulling out boxes, of shoes, a suitcase full of clothes, more shoe boxes, but not a single one of them held papers.

"Aunty Morieba," Moremi whispered as a memory nudged her mind, "I don't think we'll find the box."

Morieba looked up at her, "Why?"

"Olori Ebi took them."

Morieba expelled a sigh of disgust, "Are you sure about this?"

"Yes Aunty, it was the day after Alhaja's burial, he was carrying boxes overflowing with paper. I met him as he came out of grandma's room."

"Shit!" Morieba stood up. She suddenly beamed, "I bet he didn't find this though." She crowed and ran towards the wardrobe. She started pulling out clothes, piles and piles of expensive materials were dumped unceremoniously on the bed.

Moremi was not surprised that none of Alhaja's clothes had been touched. Nobody wanted the personal effects of a woman who died troubled.

After emptying it, she peered into the wardrobe. "Come, let me show you."

She beckoned at Moremi, they peered in. There was nothing, just a wall surprisingly bare of paint. Morieba placed her palm flat on it and slid a panel open. Behind the panel was a square shaped hole, Morieba stepped back.

"I think you should do this, after all it belongs to you."

Moremi inserted her hand into the hole and pulled out a stack of 500 naira notes, and then another stack, and another one. Just when she thought there was nothing else in the hole, her palm touched something hard and leathery. She pulled it out. It was a pouch, she pulled open the strings that held the mouth shut, and inside it were three passbooks, her mother's and grandmother's passports, three

madam cherie coco . . .

Olori Ebi paced the length of his spacious bedroom and studied, once again, the interlocking patterns of the wooden floor. Night after night, ever since that infernal girl! Sent from the pits of hell! Morieba, had come to see him about her damned business proposal! He had lost his sleep, his peace of mind.
I had it all neatly tied up. Moremi sent to Lagos, the deeds to the properties and the Will in my possession. Rents flowing into my account. A deal in the works to sell the Lekki property. Now that fucking witch wants to take it all away. She's out to ruin me!
The only thing left were the bank accounts, how to bye-pass the fucking, fussy official rules of the bank and get Alhaja's money out.
To make matters worse the stupid old woman had not used just one single bank, three damned banks, all of them greedy, none of them willing to cut a deal with me, fucking cowards! It had been 'bring one paper', after the other.
Affidavits, statements of my own account, signatures, Death certificates, letters of authorization!
He had tried to figure out a way of declaring Amope dead, but had been meeting 419's and sheer incompetents.
He was suddenly tired, he wanted some sleep, maybe his head would clear, maybe he'd be able to think better.
The best he'd been able to do were two hours, interrupted by nightmares, of Morieba chasing after him with a machete, or his debtors coming to his office to disgrace him, or having to sell the only property left to him, his father's house.
The shame, the disgrace! She wants to open my yansh in public!
He swept his hand over his head, gathering all the ill luck that might be hovering there, and snapped his fingers in the direction of the window.

A head attracting ill-luck does not belong to me.
He placed both hands on his head and blessed himself.
My head the praised, my head the worshipped.
After a few more prayers he calmed down somewhat and pulled open the drawer of his bedside cabinet, fetched a small bottle full of sleeping pills and swallowed four, dry.
The medicine had been recommended to him by the new doctor Wale had sent him to see. The man had asked him to take only two, warning him about how strong and addictive the pills were. Olori Ebi laughed.
The doctor might be well versed in the white man's medicine, but he knew nothing about the spiritual, of witches, mothers of the night, who would tie hundreds of wrappers in flight. Those who ate your arm through your brain, mothers of the earth that consumed your heart through your kidneys. Women who drank human blood for sport.
If Morieba isn't a witch how had she convinced poor, mad, Tola to give her Moremi's guardianship? How had she persuaded a woman well known for being anti-social to come out of her room, talk less of her flat? How did she manage to hide her from everybody for a whole month?
Olori Ebi grabbed the bottle of schnapps sitting on the cabinet, unscrewed the cover and gulped down a quarter of its contents in one long swallow. He knew that even if he swallowed all the pills in the small bottle, it would do nothing for him.
The only thing that can quench this fire is a bigger conflagration. I have the matches and a keg full of petrol.
The alcohol burnt its familiar route into his gullet. He lay on his bed and shut his eyes, waiting for that slowing down of his heartbeats, the soft cloudiness that inked up the eyes. He was really, truly tired.
I just want to sleep, I need to sleep, stop thinking Raufu, if I can just stop thinking for a moment.
That woman, Iya Ruka or *whatever her name is,* came yesterday, around 7pm, she came with gleeful eyes, shining teeth that had been stained brown from eating too many kola-nuts, at him. Her goitre bounced, it danced a jig around her neck.

She'd come to 'thank him' and to ask him to help him 'thank aunty Morieba'.

For the *great and bloody wonderful* aunty Morieba had told her she can move into Alhaja's house. Not only that, *the amazing and freaking marvellous* aunty Morieba had given her some money to buy more sewing machines.

Oh isn't she a sweetheart? Isn't she a hero? Shouldn't she be given a national award for being the most bleeding wonderful and damned marvellous aunty Morieba ... ever liveth?

Olori Ebi had looked at the woman with distaste. The acid in his guts burnt its way to his throat, bitter! That was how he felt. Bitter and betrayed!

When he had given Iya Ruka the keys to Alhaja's compound, wasn't it to help her? Not only would she have unsupervised access to the house, to take whatever she wanted whenever she wanted it, she was also collecting a stipend from him for the job. She was only asked to clean up, once a year, around the time of Alhaja's remembrance. Nobody questioned her about how she ran the place. But how had she repaid him? By opening the gate to that stupid Morieba and Moremi!

"Couldn't you have informed me?" He had yelled at the woman.

"But, but, sir," the woman had blabbered, "I thought you already knew. Aren't they your daughters? Moreover," she had peered at him through sly, laughing eyes, "the house belongs to Moremi and nobody in their right minds would lock a landlord out of their own premises!"

That was when he snapped. He had jumped on her with a fury that surprised even him.

Olori Ebi knew he was not a violent man. Yes, he could be cold, calculated, evil even, but his violence had never been directed at women.

Even in his former life as Raffie the Razor, he'd never raised his hand to hit a woman. It was cowards that did that, real men don't beat their women. He had his ways of dealing with women, better ways than merely beating them.

But he hadn't been able to control himself with that stupid woman. He had beaten her until she curled into herself like the cur she was. It had taken the trio of Iyawo, Quadri and Lekan to restrain him.
They should have allowed me kill to her, at least I would have rid the world of one damn ugly woman!
He knew the person to blame for his loss of control, he-knew-her-name. His palms itched as they remembered the satisfaction of slapping the woman, punching her, poking her in the eye.
"Who told you the house belongs to Moremi? Who told you that you cross-eyed, goitre infested excuse of a woman! In the days of yore, I would have sacrificed you to Ogun, because you're nothing more than meat to the gods!"
All these he had been yelling at her while Iyawo and Quadri had tried to put the woman together, they gathered her torn clothes off the floor, and hurried her through the door, while Lekan held him bound in a steel embrace.
For a brief second, Olori Ebi felt stirrings of something close to guilt, but he pushed it aside. He did feel bad though, he should not have directed his rage at her, Iya Ruka was beneath contempt. The person deserving his ire was nowhere near, Morieba!
Èsù had obviously ignored his pleas. Olori Ebi hadn't been bothered at first, he'd simply gone ahead and called the attention of other gods. After all, there was a whole pantheon of them.
He had offered alligator blood, dog meat, kola, he even killed a whole cow for Oya, the goddess of tumultuous weather. He'd tried every damn thing Baba Lalupon had instructed him to proffer as sacrifices for the gods, but so far, nothing had worked. Moriba was still strutting about town like she owned the earth, throwing parties that made the news, her guests printed in full colour in many gossip magazines.
When he had gone to her house to retrieve Tola, and Iya Tola and Wale had rained insults on her, instead of getting offended, she had merely smiled and offered them food.
The fucking witch! Does she even know how to cook?
Olori Ebi's thoughts roiled within him. The hands of the luminous clock hanging on the wall opposite his bed crept slowly, oh-so-

slowly. He followed every ticking second, 5:00, 5:01, 5:02....

Someone was banging his head with a hammer, not my head the door. As he surfaced from sleep, his eyes went directly to the clock, it was 6:23 a.m. He was too exhausted to shout, too disturbed by the constant banging on his door to ignore it and hoped whoever it was would go away. So he flung aside the bedclothes and went to pull it open. It was Lekan.

"What is it now?" He asked wearily. He felt every single day of his fifty-four years from his head to his littlest finger.

"Good morning Baami," Lekan started.

"Get to the point," He was fully awake now.

"There are two men and four police officers downstairs, they are asking for you."

Olori Ebi's first instinct was to jump through the nearest window, "Police ke?"

It took everything he had, every single will in his body not to scream those words at Lekan. He straightened up and took his hands off the door frame.

"Tell them I'll be down in a moment, take them into the parlour."

"I asked if they would like to sit down, but they refused sir."

"Just go and stay with them, except you want me to come downstairs naked. Is that what you want?" He barked the last sentence at Lekan and shut the door with a bang that echoed the collapse of his bravado. He leaned his head against the closed door, his palms clammy, he clenched them when they started shaking.

Is there going to be no end to this haunting? Did I do something to anger Èsù? Why is ill luck following me about like a fart follows its owner?

The last time he'd had anything to do with the police was about twenty-three years earlier. When he had been in the first flush of his youth, one of the fiercest armed robbers that ever terrorized the citizenry.

But it's been so long...

He sat down at the foot of the bed, he cradled his head within his arms.

Olori Ebi and his friends had been on a mission that had gone horribly wrong. The mission, like previous ones, had been meticulously planned, the insider was a well-known man who had brought successful deals to them in the past, but that last mission had been a trap.
They had the husband and his wife prostrate on the floor, the money that the man had just taken home from the bank had already been dragged out to their getaway car. But Sule, as usual, had been high and wanted to mess around with the family before they left. He had just ordered the man's houseboy to start fondling madam's breast when the police had barged in on them.
Luckily for Olori Ebi, he had been rummaging through the fridge, when he heard shots that did not sound like it came from one of their guns. They all had guns with silencers on them, but the shots were loud and sounded like assault rifles.
He had squeezed through the window and had made his escape by jumping over the fence at the back of the house.
He ran, he fast trotted, he went dumb and blind with panic, he ran without any thought as to where he was going, he had simply followed his feet. He had been mildly surprised when he found himself at Alagbado in the evening of the following day.
No it can't be that! I've not been back to Alabere since then!
He took a fear banishing breath and hurried into his clothes. He was soon threading the stairwell with heavy steps so that those waiting for him would know he did not fear them.
They were all there, in the passage-way, four uniformed police men and two in plainclothes.
"How may I help you?" He used a voice made gruffer by the huge lump of fear that had taken up residence in his throat.
One of the men stepped forward and handed him an envelope, the other one, wearing a tie that looked like it might strangle him at any moment pushed a clipboard towards him.
"Please sign here sir."
"What am I signing?" He stepped back. "You can't just barge into a man's house and order him to start signing papers!"

The policemen that had hitherto been standing around with an air disinterest stood to attention and moved towards him as one.

"You can't come into my house and start threatening me!" Even as he was shouting His bowel threatened to dislodge its contents.

The man that had handed him the letter gave a careless wave of his hand, the policemen fell back into their nonchalant attitude. Olori Ebi wasn't fooled.

"We are sorry sir, I'm a clerk from the high court and the letter you've been given is a restraining order, you can look through it, but you do need to sign here to show that you got the letter."

"You should have said all that before starting to act like commando." He stretched out his hand for the clipboard and signed hurriedly. Since they were not here to arrest him, he thought it prudent to get rid of them quickly.

After signing he stalked off to the sitting room and waited with bated breath until he heard the front door locked firmly.

He then looked at the thick envelope still clutched in his fist. He tore off the flap, wondering about its contents.

It was an officious looking document bearing the logo of an Ibadan high court. He attempted to read it but the small lettering made his eyes ache.

He pulled open the door and shouted for Quadri. He handed the letter to him, "What are they saying?"

Five minutes after collecting the envelope from him Quadri was still reading and shaking his head with what Olori Ebi suspected was amusement.

"When will you finish reading this thing?" He snapped impatiently, "Why are you reading this thing as if it's a love letter? Just tell me everything in one sentence!"

Quadri folded the document neatly and replaced it in the envelope. "The long and short of all these Baami, is that the court is ordering you never to go near any of Moremi's property again, that henceforth all rents would be paid into one account that has been opened for her."

Olori Ebi smirked, her property, if they are hers where are the title deeds?

He had suspected that this day would come, since that witch had refused to die. He just hadn't thought it would be this soon. He had assumed he would at least have some time to gather his arsenal.

"So what are you going to do now Baami?" Quadri asked quietly.

"Get out of here!"

As Quadri shut the door he jumped out of his seat and paced a familiar path on the floor. Quadri's question went round and around his head.

What are you going to do now?

Olori Ebi thought long and hard, he considered pulling out his joker, but it isn't over until it's over. He still had one more card to play; there is a saying about people in glass houses and stones, yes? He would play his final card and get a guarantee that Moremi would never mess with him again.

He fished his phone out of his pocket and placed a call to Madam Cherie-Coco.

"Razor," a voice made hoarse by too many cigarettes came over the speaker.

He could picture her. Cherie with a stick of cigarette dangling off her dark lips, those lips that used to do things to him in the days when jungle dey mature.

Her skin bleached to the endodermis by way of a special chemical bath she took about three times annually and refusal to leave her house during the daytime.

Her overflowing curves seated comfortably in a giant recliner she had specially made. The phone clenched in her fist. Knuckles that had stubbornly refused all attempts at being bleached contrasting with the rest of her.

He hated that Cherie still called him by his old name, a name he had given up along with his guns and machetes. But there was nothing he could do about it, he and Cherie went way back, they had eaten palm oil together, they had drunk wine from the same calabash…

That doesn't mean she shouldn't let the past remain dead.

He decided to let it slide, as usual.

"I have a job for you," he whispered. He threw the doors open to ensure none of his children were eavesdropping.

"Why else would you be calling me?" Madame Cherie Coco drawled, "to tell me you want to marry me?"
She laughed, a deep laughter that reflected her greedy appetite for life. Making mockery of those days when Razor had been so desperate to marry her.
He had been one of her many lovers, he had assumed, naively, that she would settle for him because he was the only one allowed to spend the night in her home, the others she usually sent away.
He remembered that same laughter on the day he returned from Alagbado and had snuck into her house at Alabere early one morning. He told her of his plans to straighten out his life, to make her his wife.
"I should give up my career and come and marry you?" She had roared. "I'll lend you a coin honey, the police are searching for you, they've been here twice."
Olori Ebi had a word with his feet.
Although he had given up on the idea of marrying her. He had not stopped using her to carry out certain jobs.
Cherie Coco was a professional to the core, a man!
"I want you to do a setup for me. Her name is Morieba Alagbado."
A long silence.
"Are you talking about Morieba Alagbado the business mogul or someone else?"
"We are talking about the same person." Olori Ebi snapped in annoyance.
"You must be kidding me," She tittered. "Do you even know the woman you're asking me to set up?"
"Oh yes I do. You may not know this, but she's my sister's daughter and she grew up in my house. I know her secret Cherie that's why I'm calling you," he lowered his voice, "she likes women."
Cherie sighed loudly into the phone.
"That shouldn't be too difficult. How does she like them?"
"She likes them in their late twenties, tall, bookish, dark-skinned. She likes them very pretty. I want pictures, better still, videos, as many as possible."

"You're going to pay heavily for this Raufu."
"Don't I, always?"

season 5
what lies beneath
(2012-2013)

fugue

Rita ran downstairs to meet Wale, as she had been doing for the past three weeks. Mummy Tobi was upstairs, making dinner and getting the children ready for bed. She smiled at him as he alighted from his car.

"You're welcome darling," She leaned in for a kiss.

"Thanks Tola," he gave her a quick peck on the lips.

"How are the children?" He asked as she took his briefcase from him. She smiled at him playfully, flirtatiously, "They are fine. They're looking forward to going to Kemi's place for the weekend."

He frowned, "I don't like the idea of the children going away again. Didn't you guys just return from Ibadan?"

"Haba, its Christmas time." She said as they climbed up the staircase. "Kemi wants them to get to know their cousins. They'll be back home by Sunday."

"I still don't like the idea."

Rita pushed open the door to the apartment, it was replete with the smell of vegetables lightly steamed in a locust bean, smoked fish, palm oil, bell peppers and onions - Wale's favourite soup.

Mummy Tobi was magic in the kitchen. Her chubby fingers would measure out precise amounts of ingredients, while she danced to the songs coming out of the small CD player she had installed in the kitchen as soon as she started working for them.

Wale had not been pleased about the music, he had not been pleased that the woman had been sent to them by Morieba, but more than that, he hated that Mama Tobi treated him with a cold indifference.

lakiriboto chronicles

She would smile at him politely anytime they came in contact, but that was where it ended. She never responded directly to any of his instructions, neither would she answer any question that was not related to work, but the woman was magic in the kitchen.

Wale drew in a deep breath as he shut the door behind him.

"I'm suddenly very hungry. What are we having with the efo?"

"Amala."

Rita allowed Wale to precede her into their room. She helped him with his clothes, she took off his socks, his shoes. She fetched a bowl of warm water from the bathroom, washed and massaged his feet.

They had neither discussed Ibadan nor the events that led up to it. They were back to regular programming, at least he was back to regular programming.

Rita was a good and obedient wife. She returned from Ibadan with her twelve yards of wife material intact. She rose early in the mornings, took long, languorous baths. She dressed in the clothes bought for her, all ruffles, pleats and flounces. She wore waist length weaves, natural hair imported from India, rumoured to be stolen from altars of Indian gods. She attended to his every need, obeyed every instruction, fussed over the children.

Being a good wife was a chore Rita enthusiastically threw herself into.

That night, after dinner, she curled into him, as they sat on the couch watching TV with the children. He pushed her away, it was too hot for cuddling, he said, but Jesutitofunmi should come and sit next to him.

"I'm a big girl now, Daddy. It's only babies that cuddle with their dads," she said.

Jesutitofunmi was a good and obedient daughter. She was growing into a lanky, self-contained pre-teen. She would no longer tolerate nonsense from her dad.

Jesutitofunmi's relationship with Rita had changed too, they spoke frankly, openly, about what had happened. They talked about her siblings, how to protect them, for daddy could not be trusted.

What daddy did was horrendous.

She had a check-up in Ibadan, there were no physical marks of that night and the nights that led up to it. But she still woke up in the night, sweating and crying.

Rita hardly ever slept, she would sit with her daughter and hold her until she fell asleep again.

Jesutitofunmi caught her mum's eyes, Rita nodded. She rose from her seat and smiled at her daddy. "I think we should go to our room now."

That night, after the lights were out, and the house was sleeping, Rita curled into him again. There was electricity, PHCN had been generous, but Wale hadn't. He had turned his back on her. She spooned him.

He was out first thing the following morning. A doctor's life you know, always busy, always on call. She'd checked his schedule, he wasn't on call till around 1p.m.

"You'll come home tonight, I have a surprise for you," she whispered as she handed him his briefcase.

Kemi came for the children around 11a.m. she looked around in amazement. "You've had the apartment repainted!"

"I had it done when I returned from Ibadan," Rita said shyly. "I actually chose the colours and painted it myself."

She showed her round the apartment, she'd done it up in pastels. Gone were the loud oranges and greens. She stripped off the garish paint with turpentine. Her walls were now painted in swirls, whorls of cream with a touch of blue and lilac. On the sitting room wall you could almost see the face of a woman emerging from the whorls. It was Tola's face, she mimicked, in the painting, the way she was hiding herself in plain sight, in real life.

"This is nice!" Kemi peered at the wall.

"Come, let me show you something," Rita pulled Kemi after her, through the kitchen, where Mummy Tobi was making magic with beans, crayfish, palm-oil, pepper, plantain and Abba.

The winner takes it all
The loser has to fall

She pushed open the door to the room off the kitchen, the room that still smelt faintly of Moremi and Kudirat, but more strongly of paint and turpentine.

She had turned the room into a jungle. The painting ran from wall-to-wall, ceiling to floor - of thick bushes, trees, vines, twinning themselves around the trees, dangling over the bushes.

She pulled the window blinds shut and switched off the light, there were red eyes, and blue eyes, and black-brown shinny eyes, peering at them from the jungle.

"I'm speechless," Kemi breathed, "I didn't know you could paint Tola."

"It's Rita," She smiled at Kemi as she switched the light back on. "This is Rita. Tola can't draw a crooked line, but I can paint."

Kemi's expression did not change, "Rita, you're a fantastic artist!"

"Thank you so much." She beamed at her sister.

Kemi understood and that was more than enough. They returned to the sitting room.

"So where are the children?"

"They've gone to buy some things from the supermarket down the road," Rita said, "Ngozi, my neighbour's housemaid, is such a gem, she's been coming around to help with them since we returned from Ibadan."

"Oh good," Kemi sat down.

"The funniest thing is that she's stealing from me."

Kemi was shocked. "What? You know this and you're allowing her into your home? I sent my last housemaid away because she was stealing milk. I mean, powdered milk for heaven's sake!"

"Ngozi only steals medicine." Rita laughed, "It's weird really, she'd steal my contraceptives and the multivitamin pills. I let her. On all other counts she's a very good girl."

"Talking about medicine," Kemi pulled a small envelope out of her bag, "here's the lab result for the pills you asked me to help you check. They are all depressants, where did you get those pills from?"

Rita was not surprised.

"Hmm? I thought they were anti-depressants, I found them in the medicine cabinet."

Rita scrutinized the list Kemi had given her, the names corresponded with the names of the 'anti-depressants' Wale claimed had been recommended to her at the hospital.

Blue pills, pink pills, aquamarine pills, rounded pills, square pills, push-you-under pills, they are benzodiazepines, zyprexa, Seroquel...

Tola helped Rita pull herself together. Even in her hidden state she helped Rita to stay grounded. Rita was the Sàngó to her Oya, Rita was Tola, half of a whole.

"Rita! Rita!" Kemi was shaking her.

Rita blinked, "What?"

Kemi returned to her seat, "You went out for close to five minutes."

"Sorry about that, I was thinking about some things." She lifted up the sachet of 'contraceptives' she'd been using religiously for close to eight years and no longer wondered about her emptiness. "So this is a depressant too, I actually thought they were contraceptives."

She turned the medicine around and tried to read the small print, but it no longer mattered, "Now I know why that girl has been stealing the medicine."

She and Kemi burst into laughter. There's just no telling what people could get high on.

"Thanks sister." Rita folded the paper and placed it in her pocket. "What about that psychiatrist I asked you to help me to find? Dr. Adejana."

The children burst into the sitting room, all sweaty and out of breath. They were carrying shopping bags full of snacks, and toiletries. Ngozi was hot on their heels.

"Stop running around, you're going to hurt yourselves!"

"Good afternoon, Aunty Kemi." Jesutitofunmi ran to her aunt and hugged her. Kemi pulled her onto her lap and tickled her.

Rita scrutinized Ngozi's face, the girl looked animated, not like someone who was taking depressants. Rita wondered.

"Me too! Me too!" Jesuwalaye was struggling to pull his sister off Kemi's lap "tiku me, tiku me, tiku me too anti."

"Okay children, go and pack your bags!" Kemi shooed them off.

"Our bags are already packed, let's go and bring them."

Jesutitofunmi grabbed her siblings and ushered them towards their bedroom.

"Aunty, I will help them take their bags downstairs, but I have to return home, my Oga say I shull come." She leaned confidentially towards Rita and whispered, "You know say my Oga no well."

"Ngozi, thank you so much." She exchanged a look with Kemi, the two women grinned at each other.

All the noise diminished as the children and their bags were packed into Kemi's car.

"About the Dr Adejana, she works at Yaba Psychiatrist Hospital, do you want to book an appointment with her?" Kemi said as she started the car.

war games

Wale didn't get home until 12p.m. Mummy Tobi had closed since 7p.m. - another thing Wale didn't like about her.

Rita met him at the door, he reeked of alcohol. He stared at her like he had never seen her before. He probably had not.

She was wearing a school uniform, it belonged to either Kudirat or Moremi. The uniform was tight on her, in the armpit, across unfettered breasts that jiggled underneath the thin clothe. It was tight across her butt and rode up on her hips. She had her hair matted backwards, a style called kolese, her face inexpertly painted.

"Why are you dressed like this?" He asked, eyes leaving butterfly touches on her lips, breasts. They caressed the flare of her hips and lingered, longingly, on the blood red high heeled shoes on her feet.

Rita shifted, pushing her breasts forward, Wale backed off, a little.

"Remember the games we used to play when we were newly married?"

Nothing of the coy Tola showed through her voice.

His gaze was back on her face, on the black lipstick smeared on her upper lips and the underside, the eye-pencil drawn on thickly.

"But you didn't like playing those games," His eyes questioned her.

"I have decided I like them now." She grabbed him and hauled him closer. "You haff been a fery naughty boy."

"Are you sure you're up for this?" He tried to shift out of her steely grip, Rita had never seen him so unsure before. She responded with a hard slap across his cheek. "Don axe me question! You haff been a naughty boy!"
"But wait..."
She didn't, she hauled him across the sitting room into their bedroom.
He was still babbling. "We need safe words and the toys that would be used should be prepared well ahead and..."
His words dried up as Rita dropped him. She threw the bedclothes off displaying the line-up she had for him.
She pushed him hard against the wall, Wale smiled, that sharky smile she hadn't seen on his face since the early days.
"Don't open that your dirty mout and be tawkin to me!" She kissed him, hard.
She grabbed his arms and pinned them above his head. Desire coursed through her as she drew in his tongue, bit his lips, then kissed him until his eyes rolled into his head. She would conquer him today.
By the time she was done with him, he was leaning limply against the wall.
She stepped back from him. "Off your clothes!"
He straightened away from the wall, the shit eating grin was back on his face. "So you finally came to your senses, I should have sent you to Ibadan earlier."
His words plunged a knife into the open wound of her heart. She gave him a resounding slap that sent his head snapping back.
"If you open dat your dirty mout again, I go show you pepper! Just off am!"
She turned her back to him, squeezed the tears that had sprung into her eyes back and pulled herself together. She looked grimly at the toys that used to give her horrors.
Tie me up!
Tie me down!
Whip me harder you coward, whip me!
Leather whip, handcuffs, ropes, dog collar, chain, strap-on.

lakiriboto chronicles

Wale had tried everything, in their early days, to convince Tola to play his games.
Sex is a power game and I want to be your slave.
He liked role play. He wanted to be whipped, gagged, humiliated. But like the baby she had been, she had stubbornly refused to participate. Fear instilled in her by her mother, about how dirty sex was and how whoreful women who participated enthusiastically in the act were, paralysed her.
Rita, on the other hand, did not have any problems playing power games in the bedroom.
She had had time to practise in the past year. In darkened rooms, with masked men that smelt of dirt and desperation.
She knew all about desires that could not be discussed openly. She had gotten drunk on the power that came with having total control over someone else's pleasure, the power that came with getting paid for it.
She knew about trust, safe words, boundaries... but Wale's sickness had nothing to do with his BDSM fantasies, he did not deserve boundaries, or safe words.
He was about to descend into the depths of hell he had spent all their years together, pushing her into, the depths of darkness he had nearly pushed their daughter into.
Tonight was not about pleasure, it was about punishment.
She turned to face him, his shirt was lying in a white pool on the floor, his red tie flung across it.
"Undo your pants, slowly."
Wale looked into her eyes as he took off his belt, unzipped his fly, and stepped out of his pant, his boxers were rolled down his hips, his turgid penis sprang out and nodded at her.
Rita snapped the whip she'd been hiding behind her back.
"Kneel down!"
"Anti Rita please don't beat me," Wale fell into character. "I promise to be a good boy."
"You be stubborn boy!" She swished the whip through the air. "I say kneel down there!"
He knelt on the floor, a bit awkwardly.

"Now raise your hands up."
"But that's not how we play..."
"Shut up!" Rita raised her voice. "Turn around and bend over!"
He did, going on all fours. Rita swiped his butt with the whip. "You like this don't you?"
"No, no, I don't like it!" Thwack!
"You wan make I stop?" Thwack!
"No, no, please don't stop!" Thwack! Thwack!!
"You be useless man, you no get respect for your elders!"
Rita picked the dog collar off the bed and locked it around his throat. "I go tish you respect today." She picked the handcuffs off the bed. "But first, I go arrest you for naughtiness." She leaned close to him, "Shebi you want make I handcuff you." He nodded. She backhanded him. "You can't talk, abi?"
"Yes," he choked out, "this thing is a little too tight."
She knelt down beside him, her clothed breasts close to his face, she'd not taken her bath that morning, so she'd smell ripe for him. He drew in a deep breath.
"But you like it don't you? You like my smelly armpits." She lifted up her arm tearing the uniform in the process, exposing her unshaven armpit and the side of her left breast. She leaned in closer to him, he lifted up his head and sniffed. "Because your housemaids they used to smell, those ones that would punish you and fuck you!"
She bared her teeth at him as she snapped the cuffs on his wrists, "You like being fucked by housemaids don't you?"
"Yes, Anti Rita." He said as he went on all fours.
Thwack! The whip went, thwack! Thwack! He cried out.
"You're really a worm, despicable, dirty, the lowest of the low."
"Please don't beat me too hard anti Rita, I'm sorry."
"Do you want me to stop?" Thwack thwack! He was hard, his penis had grown longer, thicker.
"I can see that your one eyed snake is nodding," she chuckled.
She took the rope off the bed and wrapped it tightly around his ankles.
"What are you doing?"
"Shut up! You've been a naughty boy and I go punish you today!"

lakiriboto chronicles

Rita was a broken record.
"But that's not how it's done..."
She swiped the whip across his back and watched as a welt grew out of his skin, "Don't you ever tell me what to do again!"
She grabbed the collar, his neck snapped back, she tightened it a little more and smiled as he winced.
He slumped on the floor. Rita increased the volume of the music that had been playing in the background, fetched her reefer and a bottle of vodka, she smoked and took a pull from the bottle. Wale started coughing as the smoke thickened, so she loosened the collar a little and poured some vodka down his throat.
Then she lit the wrap of smack she had specially made for him and held it for him as he puffed on it. His eyes were soon clouded over.
"Get back into position."
As Wale struggled back to his kneeling position, she put out her reefer and his, took another shot of vodka and picked up the whip.
"You are a dirty boy, that's why your housemaids used to fuck you!"
Thwack! Thwack! Thwack! Thwack!
"Are you ready to take your medicine now?"
He nodded.
"I don tell you say make you no dey nod again!" Rita suddenly felt a rush of desire, her nipples tightened and she went damp between her thighs.
"You want your medicine now?"
"Yes."
She slapped him so hard he fell on the floor.
She leaned towards him, so he could see the burning hatred in her eyes.
"Yes who?"
"Yes, anti Rita,"
Tola reached out for the strap-on. She had ordered it off the internet the week after she returned from Ibadan. It was thick, a whopping 15 inches of plexi-glass. It was ridged. It curved wickedly, a scimitar.
She dangled it in front of his face, "You want some of this don't you?"
She moved it closer to his lips, his tongue snaked out and touched the tip, she pulled it away, he stretched his neck and tried desperately to

touch the tip of the dong with his tongue again. His face was awash with tears and mucus.

She pulled her gown up and bent over him, so he could smell her essence, his tongue reached for her clitoris. She allowed him to tongue her a little, when she started enjoying it too much she slapped his face and pushed his head away. He watched her as she strapped the dong on, he was panting like a puppy, she held his head back and pushed it into his mouth, he slobbered all over it. "Suck it, suck my dick, you dirty whore."

She pulled it out of his mouth and stood in front of him while she slathered the lubricant all over the dick.

"Did your housemaids fuck you with this?"

"Not rubber, they used candles," he sniffed.

"Me I go fuck you with my thick dick, I go fuck you wella."

She fetched the whip again, thwack, thwack, on buttocks that bore the imprint of previous lashes. She got the lubricant and spread it over his buttocks, she gentled her touch as she got to the butthole, he was moaning.

"Shut up! Shut up dia! You want make I stop? If you want my dick, you go take am quietly! Stop screaming like a bitch on heat!" She slapped his ass.

"I'm your bitch anti Rita, I'm a dirty boy, I want to be your bitch, please." He was sobbing his pain, his pleasure.

He got into position, his butt up in the air, his chest on the floor. He was clenching his butthole, his cock rigid, like it would burst at any moment, spilling his seed all over the floor.

She was poised at the edge of his hole, he was pleading, begging her, to start, to stop, to do something, please, please, please...

She slid into him in one fluid motion, shouting in triumph as she slid home. She could feel her penis, its thickness, his tightness, the wall of his hole as it clenched round the 15 inches dong. Wale was moaning, underneath her... *my bitch, my fucking bitch.*

She thrust into him, hard.

Rita rode Wale, she rode him like a horse, she rode him as she had ridden so many men in whorehouses, tiny cockroach infested rooms at Omidun, in Bariga, on Lagos Island.

He shouted as he came, he slumped on the floor, panting from exhaustion.

voyeur

Kudirat was in Morieba's dressing room, her favorite part of the house. A space where she unleashed her imagination and dreamt dreams of a future that was coming into sharp focus- scary, exciting.
Sometimes she simply sat on the rug, staring at her reflection in the mirror, Narcissus.
She would study the lines of her face, marvelling at how her skin had cleared up. Sometimes she snapped photographs for her Instagram page, taking several postures, puckering up her lips.
She spent hours on YouTube learning how to apply make-up professionally, to highlight, glow up - she was a slay queen and she intended to wear that crown for as long as she wanted.
Sometimes she just lay on the floor listing all the changes a few months had wrought in her life.
Nobody knew she used the room, it was her secret, something she didn't share with Moremi.
She'd gone into the dressing room that morning to reflect on school, about rubbing shoulders with people she used to envy and admire as they drove past her in their shiny cars. Now she was the one being driven around, in shiny cars.
She took a couple of pictures, uploaded them, laid back on the rug and started imagining how Europe would be like.
Morieba was taking them on a holiday trip and since the day she'd informed them about this fact Kudirat hadn't been able to sit still. Her heart jumped at the slightest noise, her anxieties increased. What if something bad happened and the trip had to be cancelled?
She was still deep in contemplation of all the things that could go wrong when she thought she heard a noise. She jumped off the floor and made to leave the room.

As she was about to step out of the dressing room, the door that led into the bedroom was pushed open. She froze at the threshold as Chinwe and Morieba stumbled into the room, giggling and shushing each other, they looked drunk.

Chinwe was Morieba's young friend. She was in Ibadan for her youth service and had nowhere else to stay so Morieba had offered her a room. She had been living with them since November.

A quiet mouse of a girl who always had her head buried in a book. The girl tried to be nice, but Kudirat had the impression that she was a loner.

Why is aunty Morieba kissing Chinwe?

Kudirat could not tear her eyes away from the two women kissing each other feverishly a few feet away from her. They were so into each other that they didn't even sense that there was someone else in the room with them.

Morieba's full lips would slide over Chinwe's; their tongues would entwine. They'd come up for air, look into each other's eyes, smile and then start again. Morieba would suck Chinwe's tongue into hers, Morieba's hands were mimicking her tongue, they were gliding over Chinwe's back, cuddling her buttocks, those long fingers were splayed over Chinwe's buttocks. They moulded the plumpness. Chinwe was trying to reach round Morieba's width, her hands were caressing Morieba's back.

The women danced, one step forward, one step backward. Their hands glided, slid, caressed, grabbed, squeezed. Their tongues engaged in a playful duel.

Kudirat was frozen to the spot, saliva pooling in her mouth. Her mind was filled with the image of the two women — of Chinwe sliding her fingers into Morieba's hair to pull her closer to her face.

Morieba feathered kisses down her throat, her shoulders. She slid the thin straps of the blouse off Chinwe's shoulders. She was wearing a brown, lacy bra that matched her skin tone.

Morieba took her time, kissing the plump mounds created by the push-up bra. Chinwe moaned deeply in her throat as Morieba dragged the blouse down and reached round to unclasp her bra.

She didn't allow the bra to fall to the floor, she cupped both bra and breasts in her palms and continued feathering kisses on her breasts.

Chinwe's fingers were tangled in Morieba's hair. She was breathing through her mouth, her eyes were shut, her head thrown back. In spite of the air-conditioning, a light film of perspiration glistened on her face.

By the time Morieba dipped her head lower to take one of Chinwe's stiff nipples in her mouth, Kudirat felt damp between her legs.

She clasped both hands to her mouth but did not move from that spot. She had completely forgotten how easily she could be discovered, all they had to do was to look to their left. Her eyes were fastened on the glistening nipple. She had never seen anything so beautiful.

Kudirat had seen her parents having sex before. In the middle of the night, when they thought she and her brother were asleep.

Baami would be on top of Maami, grunting away.

She had watched a lot of porn on her phone, and those of friends in school. Porn made her uncomfortable, giggly.

But nothing had ever turned her on so much that she wanted to lie down and touch herself. She wanted to grind her hand between her thighs, she wanted to sigh and moan as Chinwe was presently moaning.

Chinwe's blouse and skirt were pooled on the floor at her feet. She was wearing one of those non-existent panties that was nothing more than a bit of string in-between your buttocks.

Morieba was down on her knees, feathering kisses down Chinwe's stomach, towards the panties. Her hands splayed over the buttocks, squeezing them.

Chinwe's knees buckled, Morieba lifted her off her feet and carried her towards the bed, away from Kudirat's greedy eyes.

Kudirat snapped out of her trance. She backed into the dressing room until she felt the edge of a shelf on the small of her back. She slid to the floor bonelessly and tried to sort out her feelings.

The first thing she needed to do was sort out how to get out of that dressing room without being discovered. She sent a heartfelt prayer to Oya for guidance and fetched her phone from the pocket of her gown.

As she switched the phone on several messages came in all at once, she muted the ping! ping! All the messages were from Moremi. She hit the chat head and typed furiously.

Moremi: *Where the fuck are you? I've been searching for you all over the house. (12:15pm)*

Kudirat: *You have to help me, I'm in Aunty Morieba's room. I'll explain everything to you later. Please don't ask me how, just find a way to get Aunty Morieba and that Chinwe girl out of her room (2:24pm)*

Moremi: *What is going on? (2:24pm)*

Kudirat: *Please don't ask questions now, you have to think of something that's important enough to get Aunty Morieba out of her room. (2:24pm)*

She crawled on all fours and returned to her former position at the dressing room door. She craned her neck around the doorframe.

Morieba was kneeling on the floor, Chinwe was on the bed, her thighs thrown wide open, she was using her arms to support herself, Morieba's head was buried between Chinwe's thighs. Chinwe was moaning.

Moremi: *And how am I supposed to do that? (2:30pm)*

The message came in just as Kudirat crept back inside the dressing room.

Kudirat: *They are still at it, please just come and do something.(2:40pm)*

Moremi: *What are you on about? (2:45pm)*

Kudirat: *I promise to explain everything, can you just come and knock on the door? Pretend that you have a headache or you're having one of those existential crisis those ajebutters in the school are always talking about.(2:45)*

Moremi: *But I don't even know what an existential crisis is(2:45)*

Kudirat: *I'm dying here Moremi, please have a whatever-you-know crisis, just come now, please I owe you one. I owe you plenty. I will give you all my money (2:46pm)*

Moremi: *You have money? Where did you find it? How much is it?(2:46pm)*

Kudirat: *Please just come. (2:46pm)*

Moremi: *I'm here already. (2:50pm)*

A loud knock. Kudirat crawled quickly to the threshold.

Morieba and Chinwe were naked, both of them were on the bed. The knocking was insistent.

Chinwe jumped out of the bed, Morieba gave an exasperated snort, pulled Chinwe back and tried to kiss her. They were whispering.
The knocking didn't stop.
Morieba rose from the bed, "Who the hell is that?" She yelled as she pulled on a dressing gown.
"It's me, Moremi."
Chinwe dressed up, her pant and bra forgotten on the rumpled bed. Morieba pulled open the door, Chinwe ran out of the bedroom as if the hundred hounds of hell were snapping at her feet.
"What?" Morieba growled.
"Sorry for disturbing you Aunty but I think there's something wrong with one of the puppies..."
Kudirat ran all the way back to her room as soon as the coast became clear.
Èsù hated when their bit of afternoon entertainment was disturbed.

the denizens of alabere . . .

Olori Ebi switched on the ceiling fan as he entered his room, he threw the damp towel that had been tied around his waist on the bed, and got dressed quickly.
Today is not a day for dawdling, in and out! No time for chit-chat.
He picked a tiny oblong package off his bedside cabinet, slid an object wrapped in a red cloth out of it. A black thread was wound tightly around the cloth. He whispered instructions to it.
"You will go ahead of me, Olúgboùn - the the one that bears words in the air. You will tell Sule that everything I say is the truth, for the truth depends on the bearer of words, not on the facts. He will agree with every word that comes out of my mouth, for I have become the bearer of the truth. He will follow my orders. You are Olúgboùn, the one that carries messages through the air, and I, Raufu the son of Adetoun, am your master, for I have made sacrifices to you. So it is. Àse!"
He spat at it thrice and inserted it in the pocket of his agbada. He pulled out a drawer and picked another package wrapped in fresh

green leaves. He unwrapped it, fished out a cowry shell nestling inside and spoke to it.

"Gbetu-gbetu, the handmaiden of Olúgboùn, carry my words into the heart of Sule, the son of Bolomope."

He placed the cowry carefully in the recesses of his right cheek.

Even while he was carrying out the rituals, the shadow of doubt that had been stalking him for over a year hovered around his actions. After all the gods appear to have completely turned their backs on him.

On the other hand, the ways of the gods are unfathomable, sometimes one loses battles but at the end one wins the war. Moreover these rituals gave him boldness, and he needed all the confidence he could get.

As he descended the staircase he called Lekan.

"The car is ready Baami," Lekan appeared at the bottom of the staircase.

Olori Ebi floated out to his car on a cloud of brilliant white, dry-lace. On his head was a purple abetí-ajá that perfectly matched the colour of his pointy toed, heelless slippers.

He stood still for a moment and reveled in the shininess of the brand new Hummer he had bought after his old jalopy died.

One does not curl up and die in times of crisis. It is important to show one's enemies that they have failed.

The fact that he got the Hummer on credit was not something he worried about, providence, and lately, Morieba, had a way of covering his ass.

In spite of the fact that the girl was stubborn, hard of hearing and an arrogant witch, she'd never neglected her duty of ensuring he was well taken care of, the way Alhaja had done in her lifetime.

As he climbed into the luxurious interior of the car, his excitement dampened as he recollected his destination, his mission.

The truth was that if there was an alternative, Olori Ebi would have taken it, but that letter had forced his hand, coupled with his near empty bank account.

After collecting rents from his sister's properties for almost five years, he had realised how piddling the amount he was getting off the family lands had been. He had no intention of returning to dancing at the edge of poverty.

As the car snaked its way out of the narrow potholed roads of Idi-Ikan, onto the wider potholed road leading to Beere, an old man dashed into the road and was nearly hit by an Okada. Olori Ebi suddenly felt a fear, that the old man could be him. His discomfort was taken over by a fierce determination.

"We are going to Alabere," he grunted.

He did not ask if Lekan could find his way to Alabere. He expected all his boys to be able to make their way, even blindfolded, into places angels fear to tread. How else would they learn how to take care of themselves?

Alabere was home to thieves, drug addicts drug peddlers, sex-workers and their pimps, pick-pockets and their Fagins. This illustrious line-up included other bottom feeders of Ibadan city that kept the not-so-obviously-crooked members of the society in check.

Olori Ebi had founded the Alabere together with Sule, Cherie Coco and four other boys. If truth be told, Sule had discovered Alabere, while the others had joined in making the place what it eventually became.

The boys had met one another at a motor-park in Molete where they spent their days as conductors-cum-pickpockets; their nights were spent sleeping in parked or vandalized buses.

Sule had gotten tired of the harassment they suffered from bus drivers and having to hide from gangs of men seeking homeless children to use for rituals. He had disappeared for a whole day only to return that evening to ask the others to pool their money together.

Five teenage boys had moved into one room, in a face-me-I-face-you house, that had neither a toilet nor a bathroom.

The boys took their baths in the backyard, whenever they bothered to, and shat into polythene bags, which they threw into nearby bushes.

But it had been their home, somewhere to lay their heads, somewhere to hatch plans about how they would take over the world.

They met Cherie Coco in Alabere, their landlord's daughter. A tough muscular girl who had bullied the boys into allowing her to join their pickpocketing expeditions almost as soon as they'd moved into her father's house.

Within four years, Alabere's population had grown into a few hundred teenagers, and fewer older people. Before long 'respectable' people were moving out of the neighbourhood, making room for pimps, drug dealers, male and female sex workers and a few other nut-jobs. With them came the trade in machetes, body parts, double-edged axes (code-name Ake UTC), a few guns and ammunition.

Cherie had refused to move out with her dad, who had, by then, become so scared of her that he had not protested too much. Some nasty people claimed he was relieved that she decided to stay back.

The larger Alabere's population grew the further up the food chain Olori Ebi, (the criminal formerly known as Raffie the Razor), Sule, Cherie and the other boys climbed.

Alabere had sealed its position as the go-to place for criminals when gang wars broke out between the older warlords and the snotty-nosed teenagers, who were getting rather uppity because they had a few machetes.

Alabere was a ripening mango to be plucked before it became the meal of bush birds.

But the snotty-nosed kids were desperate, they were wild, they would rather die than let the warlords take over. They fought back with everything in their arsenal. They fought back guerrilla style.

Before they realised that the teenagers had no intention of facing them in an open battle, the warlords had lost quite a number of their men and weapons.

The government eventually waded in, levelling everything and everybody in the sight of their guns and demolition crew.

They had all gone into hiding, only to return quietly about a year later.

Within three years of their return, Alabere was once again abuzz with the activities that sent it into annals of criminal mythology — perfectly executed armed robbery operations, prostitution, drugs and begging rings, daylight fights with broken

bottles and machetes, kidnapping, arms deals and human trafficking.
Hard core fuji was the background music to their violence.
Raffie the Razor had bought his place amongst the legends with bullets and blood, until a failed robbery operation revealed the coward in him and sent him scuttling to Alagbado, and into the boring arms of respectability. From whence he metamorphosed, once again, into Raufu Alagbado.
After driving for about thirty minutes, on marginally well planned streets, Lekan emerged onto a dirt road bordered by houses in various stages of decrepitude. Lekan pulled to a stop behind a high fence that appeared to have no beginning or end. Olori Ebi alighted and walked towards the fence.
"Baami, do you want me to come along with you?"
He ignored his son and continued walking determinedly towards the fence.
Alabere was a solid square, with the well-fortified houses of the four major gang lords forming a barricade around a fiefdom built out of roofing sheets and hardboard. It was impossible to drive a car into Alabere, you either walked through the alleyways or passed through the house of one of the warlords.
It had been more than 25 years since his unceremonial exit from Alabere but Olori Ebi had no doubt about how to gain entrance.
Once he got to the fence, he inserted his thumb into a hole just off to his right and pressed it against a button. A faint click, Olori Ebi stepped back as the 'wall' opened with the loud grinding noise of half-rusted engines. He squeezed through the narrow opening and the wall ground to a close behind him.
The wall had been his brainchild. A free service provided when they had kidnapped a Lebanese construction mogul.
The compound in which he found himself was huge. The main house was farther down. On his left and right sides were bungalows, and row upon row of beer cartons.
Dark clouds were gathering swiftly in the skies, portend of heavy rain, or something more sinister ... Olori Ebi rubbed his tongue against the cowry shell in his cheek. He took his eyes off the skies and

looked towards the house. Striding towards him were three muscular men with rifles slung over their shoulders.

"Agba ki in wa l'oja," Olori Ebi called out. Almost instantly, the tallest and darkest of the men stepped forward, right arm extended.

Ori omo tuntun a wo!

Ori omo tuntun a fa'ya!

Olori Ebi grasped the arm and the two men did a complicated dance which included chest bumping, arm groping and finally the snapping of fingers.

"Welcome back home Razor," He said in a soft voice which jarred with his hard, scar ridden face, and missing eye. "Chairman has been expecting you."

He led the way and Olori Ebi followed. The two other security guards fell in step behind them.

"It's good to be home Chuks," Olori Ebi said as nostalgia and trepidation hit him with the same intensity.

It occurred to him how much danger he could be in, these men do not forgive, they do not forget.

The picture of the old man falling over in a heap after the Okada had hit him grounded him, gave him the bravery to continue walking towards what might possibly be his death. But he took one step after the other He grasped the talisman in his pocket and squeezed it tightly in his fist.

"Things have not changed much around here," he observed as they approached the one storey building. He felt a deep satisfaction when he noticed that the house had been extended in a higgledy-piggledy fashion, the extensions had obviously not seen a single stroke from an architect's pencil.

In spite of their powers they still lacked a sense of aesthetics.

"Things should not change all the time," Chuks paused and glared at him, "Raffie the Razor."

Olori Ebi's former name was a curse on his lips. He shook his head and continued on the walk. "You know it's not all of us that have the luxury of running away in times of trouble." Olori Ebi winced as he caught the shade thrown by Chuks. "We wan sabi say the tins we leave behind, when we dey inside wall, go dey when we return."

Olori Ebi clenched his jaw. He would not allow a mere henchman ruin his mission. What does Chuks know about brotherhood and loyalty? He hadn't even been there in the early days, those were the days when jungle dey mature!

As they drew closer to the main house, the door was pulled open by a tiny girl, who could not have been more than 15years, a pistol in her fist. She stared openly at Olori Ebi who stared right back at her.

She was dressed in a pair of combat trousers, in the greens of the Nigerian army and a singlet which clung to her voluptuous breasts. She reminded Olori Ebi of Iyawo, when she had been younger, before she started popping out the babies, he wondered if she would be as sweet.

They passed by a roomful of people laughing uproariously, the smell of alcohol and marijuana strong in the air.

Chuks led him up a flight of stairs. They walked down a long corridor and eventually turned left, into a room that was cool and blessedly quiet.

As Olori-Ebi shut the door behind him, the hum of an air conditioner filled his ears. In front of him was a huge mahogany table which held three laptops and an innumerable number of phones.

Sule dropped the phone he was fiddling with and widened his arms and lips in an expansive welcome gesture. "It is good to see you Razor."

Sule was a man of diminutive dimensions. His face was that of a six year old child with pink lips, a delicate nose and perfect shell-shaped ears. Whenever he bothered to smile, like he was presently doing, two cute dimples appeared in his cheeks, and his perfectly matched teeth would peep through them. His glasses gave him a bookish, introverted demeanour. However, he made up for his angelic looks by being deeply, darkly and truly evil.

"Same here Sule, same here." Olori Ebi was a bit annoyed that Sule still looked that good. Although he was dressed in a pair of torn jeans, a t-shirt, and a pair of loafers, beside him, Olori Ebi felt crude, an overbloated elephant that had seen better days.

Sule led Olori Ebi to another part of his office which held a few comfortable chairs.

"You just left us without a backward glance, but it's alright man." He flicked Olori Ebi's agbada. "You're now a proper civilian, complete with agbada and a flourishing stomach." He patted Olori Ebi's stomach.

"This, Sule," He rubbed the said stomach and smiled, "is a sign of good living. It is only the person that has a big stomach that the money would be given in big Ghana-must-go bags."

The two men laughed as Chuks picked a bottle of schnapps, still in its carton, off the small bar in one corner of the room, placed it on a tray and added two shot glasses on it. He placed the tray reverently on the glass topped table in front of the men.

Sule opened the carton, he showed Olori Ebi its unbroken seal, he then handed the bottle back to Chuks who opened it and served the men in the thimble sized tumblers.

Olori Ebi laughed to himself, if Sule wanted to poison him, a mere seal would not stop him.

"To old friendships, and running away to fight another day." He toasted Olori Ebi and downed the contents in one gulp. Olori Ebi refused to take the bait, he merely smiled and swallowed his drink.

"And to what do we owe the pleasure of your visit?" Sule asked after refilling the glasses.

"I came to see how the old place is doing." Olori Ebi said. Sule lifted an eyebrow and the two men laughed.

"It took you 25 years to come and check how we've been doing, how convenient." Sule coughed. "Tell me another lie Razor."

Olori Ebi's response was a smile.

"I do get reports about you, man." Sule continued, "I heard you're doing quite well, that you have a house full of sons."

"It is Eleduwa's doing." Olori Ebi downed his drink and poured himself another shot. He wasn't here for small talk. "Sule, I need a favour from you."

Sule smiled. "Now we are getting somewhere."

Olori Ebi did not care for his sarcastic tone but he had business, he would not engage in banter. He owed nobody an explanation, he knew those men, in his shoes they would have done the exact same thing.

"I'm looking for my sister's daughter," he continued, "and I've gathered from reliable sources that she's now living in your kingdom."

Sule leaned forward and poured out some more of the schnapps into Olori Ebi's glass.

"Her name is Amope." He ran his tongue around the cowry shell inside his cheek. "She does crack when heroin is not available. I heard she moved here about four years ago."

"Amope," Sule fingered his chin, "that name sounds familiar, Chucks!"

"My Chair," Chuks who had dematerialized immediately after serving the drinks suddenly reappeared.

"Do you know of any Amope?" Sule looked up at him.

Chuks was the registrar. He knew every single soul that lived in Alabere. He knew their real names, code names, family lineage, how much they earned, how useful they were, where they came from. He knew when it was time for them to depart from Alabere, usually feet first.

"Yes I know Amope, it's that deportee that speaks like she's the queen of England, but she earns her keep, so she's alright."

Sule turned back to Olori Ebi.

"I want her back," Olori Ebi adopted a sad mien. The bewildered uncle whose heart had been broken by his favourite niece. "She's my sister's only child and we've been searching for her since before her mother's death over seven years ago. That girl has caused so much heartbreak and sadness to her mother and the little, innocent daughter she abandoned."

Sule gave him a long, hard look. Olori Ebi squirmed. He hadn't bargained for the drama, all he wanted was in and out, no questions asked, no thinking over things. He touched the talisman in his pocket and rolled his tongue around the cowry.

"Ah, I remember Amope now, you used to bring her here when she was younger." His eyes gleamed as he gave Olori Ebi a considering look. "Seven years is a long time, why are you just coming here?" He used a finger to push his glasses back on his nose. "You know there's no junkie I can't find for you as long as she's within Nigeria. So what really happened?"

Olori Ebi's patience was at an end, he pushed his face into Sule's. "I want you to go and bring her for me."

Sule pushed him. "Back off! Who are you to just stroll in here after twenty-five years and start ordering me around?" He paused, and suddenly broke into an angelic smile. "We should be celebrating how far we've come since the last time we saw each other not fighting." He looked up. "Chucks fetch Amope and call Bashiru for me."

Olori Ebi released a pent up breath as Chucks left the room.

"Amope is actually a nice girl, I remember her quite clearly now." Sule said quietly, "poor thing, what you did to her though..."

The sins of the mother
shall be visited on the daughter
the granddaughter,
the great-granddaughter,
forever and ever amen.

The men recited Alabere's motto together, sotto voiced.

"I remember your rich half-sister, that must be Amope's mother, so she's dead. I wonder how you managed to off her without pulling a hit." He downed another tumbler of schnapps, "or maybe I shouldn't, you're still handy with poisons I suppose, cowardly shit, but whatever rocks your boat man."

Olori Ebi cursed Èsù underneath his breath, for a minute he had taken his mask off, allowed Sule under his skin, one must never be vulnerable with the enemy.

"Yes, poor Aduke died, we woke up one morning and she was dead." Olori Ebi got back into character. "But thanks be to Allah that she did not suffer for long, she left quietly. May He grant her eternal rest."

"I'm sure you're also thankful that you know her daughter is here." Sule drew closer to Olori Ebi. "So tell me Razor, why do you want her now? What changed? Seven years is a very long time, is it the signatures? Was there a Will?"

Olori Ebi narrowed his eyes and projected steel into his voice. "I did

not come here to be cross-examined Sule. I came to fetch my niece."
"Mmm, you want your junkie back, your rich junkie. Does she even know that her mother is dead?" Sule poured himself another shot.
"How much do you want?" Olori Ebi growled. He splashed schnapps into his tumbler and downed two shots in quick succession.
"Half of everything."
"You must be out of your mind."
"Ah the money must be even more than I imagined," Sule drawled.
"I'm not here to play games!" Olori Ebi's mind worked furiously. That the gbètu-gbètu did not work was clear. He waved a mental fist at the Mothers, those who killed you slowly all the while laughing with you.
"Neither am I."
Sule waited a heartbeat and then laughed, he laughed so hard tears coursed down his cheeks. Olori Ebi stared at him, the problem with people that smoke too much marijuana is that it affects their brain eventually. That's why he never touched the stuff no matter how badly he hungered for a high, he stuck to alcohol which was way better.
Sule stopped laughing as abruptly as he had started. Olori Ebi expelled an exasperated breath and growled.
"It's alright Razor, I'm not as greedy as you." He patted his arm. Olori Ebi snatched the arm out of his way. "I know you too well, the next thing you'll do after leaving this place is to go and hire somebody to kill me, or find other devious means of throwing sand in my garri." He shook his head ruefully, "And I like a quiet life, my bullets have better uses." He swept Olori Ebi a clinical look. "You look pretty unhealthy anyway."
Olori Ebi unclenched his fists.
"Here's the deal." Sule looked at him from behind the glinting glasses. "You take your niece and we'll take ten million naira when the deal, whatever it is, is done."
Olori Ebi released a pent up breath. "Highway robber!" He shouted in relief. "The one and only Sule, thief exemplar!"
Sule burst into laughter, "You don't need to sing the praises of my

lineage."

"I can't promise you ten million." Olori Ebi sobered up. "You'll definitely get eight. I don't even know the worth of my sister's properties."

"We can help you find out, you know we have the means." Sule's smile was oily.

"No, thank you very much, I can do that by myself." Olori Ebi held out his hand, Sule grabbed it and the two men did the same complicated set of handshakes he had exchanged earlier with Chuks.

Èsù grabbed a bottle of Shnapps off the cabinet and joined the men in a celebratory drink.

a cry-cry film . . .

Moremi was lying across her bed, face down, chin on the pillow, long fingers holding open the book she was reading. Kudirat was lying down beside her, one pillow tucked underneath her chin, another on top of her legs. She was reading too.

On the floor between the two girls was a plate of digestive biscuits and two glasses of orange juice.

The only sounds in the room were those of the whispery turning of paper, and the quiet hum of the air-conditioner.

They were supposed to be reading for their WAEC exams which would start in a couple of weeks. But they were tired of reading academic books and staring into the screen of their iPads. They'd sat for their IGCSCE's the previous month, and had passed with flying colours.

Kudirat more than Moremi.

The girls had agreed that Kudirat was a show off, she did not need to score all A's. She was an overachiever who wanted to show the students in their new school that just because she had spent the

better part of her life in government schools did not mean she was dumb or stupid.
It was also a form of revenge on the rich-kids for laughing at her accent.
Moremi had nothing to prove to anybody. All she wanted was to be left in peace to read, and travel, and maybe sometime in the distant future, write about her adventures. She was determined never to be pressurised to do what she did not want to do. Although she was going along with Kudirat pretending an interest in medicine, she was only doing it to keep herself occupied until she laid hands on her inheritance.
Moremi picked a biscuit and chewed it slowly as she read The Secret Lives of Baba Segi's Wives by Lola Shoneyin. She wriggled in enjoyment. She'd just turned another page when Morieba's chat head popped up on her phone.
Aunty M: Sweetheart can you kindly come downstairs immediately? And tell Kudirat not to follow you or try to snoop. (11:45am)
Moremi giggled as she read the message, Kudirat peeped over her shoulder.
"Oh, so me, I'm the snoop now, abi?" She laughed and rolled over.
"The matter that we don't want the kingpin to hear, it's the kingpin that would end up solving it."
Moremi: I'll be down in a minute(11:45am)
Morieba: I'm in the sitting room.(11:45am)
Moremi: Okay Aunty(11:46am)
She rose from the bed.
"Whatever, just don't follow me or do that sitting on the staircase and eavesdropping thing you do. Kingpin indeed, when you look more like a safety pin or an office pin."
Kudirat threw a pillow at her, Moremi dodged it, stuck out her tongue and escaped through the door as another pillow sailed her way.
She was still giggling when she got downstairs. She skipped towards the sitting room, which was off to her right and stopped cold at the door. Her face turned stiff.

Sitting down in a pool of yellow jacquard lace was Olori Ebi. The stones that dotted the lace shone even brighter than the afternoon sun pouring through the glass door that led to the verandah.

His cap was red, his smile white, his cheeks dimpled. His tribal marks, a work of art. He sat prettily like a bride about to walk down the aisle. Conscious of how good he looked.

"Ah ah, Morieba, why is this one here?" He chuckled.

Moremi was staring at him as one would a snake, with repulsion and fascination.

"Good afternoon sir." She dipped her knees and walked sideways to where Morieba was seated. She was afraid of turning her back on him. He seemed like the kind of person that would sneak up behind you and bury a knife in your solar plexus.

"Good afternoon, good girl," he bared his teeth at her. "I can see you're looking more and more like your aunty every day. See both of you are even dressed the same way, jeans and baggy t-shirts."

Moremi knew when she was being mocked. Certain people had a way of delivering the most innocent statements as an insult. She deliberately turned her back on him and leaned towards Morieba, who had been quiet throughout the exchange.

"Please sit down." She said stiffly, "Raufu Alagbado has something to say to you."

Olori Ebi looked taken aback for a moment, but he recovered quickly enough, the amiable smile back on his face.

"I've already told you everything, and I don't think that children should hear that kind of thing, our discussion is strictly for adults."

"I don't think so," Morieba said coldly. "Moremi turned 18 last week, so she is no longer a child, and since it's her grandmother's property we are talking about. I don't think it is right that we should discuss it behind her back."

"Nobody hears bad news from the mouth of a diviner." He muttered uncomfortably glanced at the shiny watch on his wrist. "See how time flies when you're enjoying yourself." He jumped out of the chair, "I think I'd better leave now."

"Sit down!" Morieba's words were crisp and dry, they bore the chill of Harmattan wind.

The hairs along Moremi's neck sprang up, she shivered in apprehension.
Morieba picked up the remote control on the low stool beside her and deliberately pressed 'lock'. The click of bolts sliding home was like a hammer.
"The doors are locked, and they won't open for the next fifteen minutes. Enough time for us to discuss this important matter that you brought to my attention this morning."
Moremi was staring at her aunt, she'd never seen her that way before. Her face was a mask of fury, her eyes shone with tears. She moved as close as it was possible to Morieba, quietly.
"I will remain standing then." Olori Ebi said stubbornly.
"It's your choice." Morieba turned her attention to Moremi.
"I have something to tell you," she said, "I should have told you before now, but I didn't think it was important. I thought I should give you enough time to get to know me and to start healing from the brutality that the man standing over there exposed you to for some years."
Moremi took her aunt's hand in hers. "You don't have to tell me anything."
"What's all these rubbish?" Olori Ebi snapped. "Morieba open the door this minute or there'll be hell to pay."
Morieba ignored him, her eyes still on Moremi. "I'm a lesbian. I know you know what that means."
Moremi shrugged.
Olori Ebi sucked his teeth loudly. "Ah! The things that these Oyinbo people have done to us is madness. See these ones behaving as if they are in one of those cry-cry films they are always showing. Maybe they'll soon start singing like those Indian film people."
Morieba stared at him blank faced all through his tirade.
"Okay, I think it's done talking."
She said after Olori Ebi fell quiet and stalked back to his seat. He sat down with such force that the leather covering of the seat squeaked in protest. She picked a folder off the table and handed it to Moremi.
"Open it."
Moremi hesitated, she knew something bad had happened. She

didn't want to know what it was.

"I said open it!"

Moremi flipped the folder open and the first thing she saw was an eight by eleven full colour picture.

A woman was lying on her back, she was stark naked. Between her thighs was another woman whose back was turned to the camera.

The woman on her back was Morieba.

The second shot showed her fucking the same woman, doggy style with a black strap-on. The next one was of her suckling on the woman's breast.

Every photograph showed Morieba naked, her face captured in different grimaces, her body in different postures.

The other woman's face was always averted, but Moremi identified the woman as Chinwe - It was in the curve of her cheeks.

"Ah, you no longer have any shame. How can you be showing these kind of things to a young girl? Isn't there a law against pornography? Don't you even feel a twinge of conscience?"

Moremi was confused. Of course she knew her aunt was gay, but why was she showing her these pictures?

"Now take a good look at the bastard sitting over there."

Moremi didn't look at the bastard, because he was not important. She closed the folder and watched her aunt who had tears streaming down her face, tears of humiliation that she was not bothering to hide.

"He said we should stop asking after your grandmothers properties, that he has all the deeds to the houses. He said you can keep the money but he's keeping the properties. He said we should have the court injunction rescinded."

Morieba's lips were trembling, she couldn't talk any longer.

Moremi took the remote from her slack fingers and pushed the button that would open the door.

Olori Ebi stomped out of the room. Neither of the women looked at him. Moremi hugged her aunt.

"He has videos, he has more pictures." Morieba blubbered into Moremi's T-shirt.

"It was Chinwe, it must be her."
She sniffled and placed her head in the comforting crook of Moremi's shoulder.
"I knew something was wrong when she left without telling anybody and her phone couldn't be reached. She stole some of my jewellery but those can be replaced, that's why I didn't say anything."
Morieba finally straightened up and wiped her face with a handkerchief she fetched out of her pocket.
"It's alright Aunty M."
Moremi placed her forehead against her aunts. She looked into her eyes and saw the hurt in them.
"I'm not crying because he threatened to publish those things in the newspaper, I'm crying because it really hurts when family members betray your trust in them. But he doesn't care that he's tearing our relationship apart. All he cares about are those houses. Why is he so desperate?"
One thing Moremi was good at was listening, so she did, to the bewilderment in her aunt's voice, the unspoken fears, the shame...
"If he told me he wanted money, I would have given it to him. Lord knows I've bailed him out of trouble enough times. He went and bought a jeep on credit, earlier this year. I've paid for the damn thing and he doesn't even know. I don't even drive a jeep."
"Heey! Aunty Morieba!"
The two women looked up, it was Kudirat.
"Did you see Olori Ebi? He just left now!" She fell quiet suddenly and walked over to where the other two women were seated.
"What is it? Tell me what happened!"
Moremi asked Morieba a question with her eyes, she nodded. Moremi handed Kudirat the folder. She glanced at the first picture, and tossed it on the floor.
"He's trying to blackmail you abi?" She smiled mirthlessly, "We will handle this!"

season 6
the trouble with being
(2013-2014)

la petite mort

If I were Tola, I wouldn't have been able to handle this. I'd be crying, I'd be so damned scared. I'm sure that by now I'd be thinking that I'm a monster. That I've crossed the boundary of being human. Like Ogun wielding my vengeful machete, or less? Subhuman, an amoeba maybe, but I'm not Tola. I am Rita and my work is never quite done. That's the trouble with being. Tola is human, soft, kind, forgiving, empathetic, depressed, powerless! Me I be Rita, I'm unforgiving, vengeful, and as petty as fuck.

Rita was practising breathing, breathing through her mouth that is. She was doing it the way she'd read about such things in books.
Like, if your house was on fire and the whole place was filled with smoke, right? You were advised to flatten yourself on the floor and breathe through your mouth. Because smoke was lighter than air, or is it denser? Whatever. The point was avoiding smoke inhalation while the fire-fighters literally walked through hell to rescue you.
Rita was not in a smoke filled room, but she believed that a fire-outbreak might be the solution to this problem called a police station.
The stink of the cell-room was bad enough to burn your throat worse than mere smoke inhalation, and that was discounting the tiny and not-so-tiny insects crawling all over you. Although those ones won't burn your throat, they only made you itch in places you didn't even know existed on your body.
She had remembered that breathing method around 12 midnight and had applied it. Although she'd been getting strange looks from her cellmates, she'd ignored them because it appeared to be

lakiriboto chronicles

working.

The air a little above her head stank, of unwashed bodies, urine, feaces, desperation... she kept her face as close to the floor as possible, to inhale a somewhat stale but stink free air.

Maybe it's my imagination, don't I stink just as badly? How long have I been here?

She sniffed the air low to the ground again and sniffed her armpit. She was still making comparisons between her stink, the stink of the room and that of the air close to the floor, when the sound of iron bars being pushed open reached her ears.

She noted, through the corner of her eye, that some of her cell-mates ran over to the gate, probably hoping somebody had come for them. Poor fools!

They complained bitterly as they were roughly shoved out of the way by two policemen.

"That's her over there," a familiar voice said from beyond the bodies clustering up the door.

Rita held her breath as she craned her neck to see if it was the same policeman that had been at the flat, with so many others, yesterday? Whatever - after Mummy Tobi had made the call.

The voice had ordered her steps all through yesterday.

'Wear something. Stand over there! Sit down there! Don't touch anything! Take off your belt!

Rita had been shell-shocked, so much so, that she dumbly followed all his orders, as dumbly as Tola would have.

Honestly I didn't know people died that messily!

She'd assumed it would be like in the movies. In movies people died prettily, their limbs arranged just so, their eyes shut neatly, they didn't drool or pop their eyes out at you!

Except in some Nollywood movies, but even then, those badly acted deaths were still prettier than the horror of yesterday — Or is it the day before? And the actors didn't spend an inordinate amount of time clawing at their throat. The horror! The horror of his long, lingering death!

It haunted her, the way he had been struggling, screaming silently because the collar had been too tight, it had cut off his voice as well as his air supply.

He nearly got her at some point, she had been studying the faces he was making. Thinking about how he was wasting the little bit of air he had left by struggling so hard- he should just have died quietly, there had been no need for all that drama, it hadn't saved him anyway…but Wale had to be a drama queen till the bitter end.

Rita had chosen to see his death throes as the ultimate ecstasy. Didn't the French call it the little death? La petite mort!

"Convess, convess now! How did you keel your horzeband?'

Who said that to me?

"What did you do with this tin?"

"Why do you use this rubber penis for?"

"Hey you!" The policeman that had opened the door yelled in her direction.

Rita tried to remember who he was. Hadn't he been in a dark room with me yesterday wearing an absurd pair of sunshades? Oh . . . it wasn't him, it was the other detective, the one that had threatened to bring out the 'inszrumens of tawshur' if I don't cooperate.

Rita decided to stand up, but she had to hold her breath first- 20,19,18,17– her throat started to burn, 15,12,10,9 –

"Hey you on the floor! Come here before I count to three!"

"I'm already counting down you stupid!" She jerked away violently as the young lady who had been sitting dejectedly beside her (all day? All night? One never knows when everywhere is so damn dark!) touched her arm. The touch had been a fleeting, butterfly one, but felt like a hammer against Rita's skin.

Without glancing in the girl's direction Rita jumped off the cold cement floor and made for the exit. The other inmates made way for her, their eyes hungrily envious of this fleeting chance to leave the dank, dark, stinking, congested cell.

"Your arms!" The policeman barked.

"My arms?"

He clasped a pair of cuffs on her wrists with a fluidity that she admired. "Go with him." He used his chin to point at another policeman who was standing off to one side in the passageway.

A babble of voices were raised as he re-locked the door.

Rita followed the other policeman down the dark and narrow passageway. The whole place stank of unwashed bodies, urine and faeces. It stank of desperation and despair.

She wouldn't want them to think she was crazy, that was why she resisted the urge to go down on all fours, breathing in the air close to the floor.

They finally emerged into a room flooded with so much sunlight that Rita had to use her arms to cover her face. When she lowered them she was standing by the 'counter' — an ugly concrete slab. It looked more like a slaughter house slab than the worktop it was pretending to be.

Rita took a deep appreciative breath, a marginally clean one, as her eyes got used to the light.

On the other side of the slab were her mother, Kemi and Morieba. The three women looked harried, anxious. She wanted to smile at them, but her mouth felt filthy, so she kept her lips in a straight line.

"There she is," Iya Tola announced unnecessarily as the women crowded the slab.

"Don't come and be running up and down here! This is a police station, not a race course." A policewoman who had been hitherto picking her teeth and gossiping with one of her colleagues barked.

"My dear, please don't be angry. We came to see my daughter. God will not let the thing that happened to her happen to you…"

Rita swore underneath her breath as Iya Tola launched into a long recital of woes that could befall the unwary, praying fervently for the policewoman.

"Are you alright?" Kemi asked her.

"No, I'm not," Rita lifted up the corners of her lips.

"You will be fine," Morieba reassured her, "We've come to see if we can make your stay here as comfortable as possible."

Rita shook her head, she did not want to be comfortable. There was no way being denied your freedom could be made comfortable. She needed to see an end to all these. She needed to hold Tola off for as long as possible, so she wouldn't come and ruin things or have to bear the pain. Tola was delicate.

That's another problem with being me. Tola can sleep, I can't. This body doesn't want to sleep, but it needs to sleep.

"The DPO will see you now," the policeman who'd fetched her from the cell was standing next to her, the other one who'd delivered her to the counter had disappeared.

"Thank you officer," Kemi smiled at him. "Which way are we going?"

"Come through this side," the policeman indicated an opening beside the counter and the wall. Kemi rushed through and wrapped Rita in an awkward hug that had a lump crawling into her throat.

Gosh! To be loved unconditionally.

Morieba patted her on the back.

As Iya Tola joined them, she looked at Rita through mournful eyes, eyes full of patience and longsuffering.

Tola was her Cross, and she would bear it– and she would show the world– her Cross.

Rita side-stepped the woman's attempt to touch her. Iya Tola clasped her hands to her breasts as silent tears flowed down her cheeks.

They were in the DPO's cramped office. The man was rotund. His stomach flourished so much that it was squeezed tightly against the table behind which he was seated. The table itself was overflowing with papers – some had fluttered to the floor when he sat down.

On the wall, behind the DPO were two framed pictures, one of the state governor and the other of the president of the Republic of Nigeria. One was smiling, the other looked as if he was being given an aenema.

"Please, please, sit down," The man smiled as if they were there on a social visit. "Mrs. Alagbado, thanks so much, I got the package that you sent to me." He directed his words at Morieba.

Morieba and Kemi sat in the two spare chairs in front of the table while Iya Tola and Rita took up positions in different corners of the room. The policeman hovered at the door.

"Sergent Limba, please leave that door!" The DPO barked. "Go and check why they've not turned on the gen. It's too hot in here."

"But sir, what about her?" Sergeant Limba pointed at Rita.

"You must be very stupid! Does it look like she would run away from here?"

The DPO had barely finished speaking when the yellow bulb dangling above them flickered into life. He turned on the fan, circulating more of the hot air coming in through the tiny windows in his office.

He dragged a folder towards him and flipped through it. His lips moved as he read the contents. After a while he sniffed and looked up at Morieba.

"Who's this?" he used his chin to point at Kemi.

"This is Kemi Lawanson, she's Tola's sister, and the other woman is Tola's mother."

Rita looked at Kemi Lawanson. Tola's sister. Yes, of course. The dense fog that had clouded her brain lifted.

"This report says your sister killed her husband on the 5th of February."

"I'm sure it also said that it was under unusual circumstances."

The room was enveloped by an embarrassed silence.

The DPO cleared his throat, and snuck a look at Rita, "Yes, yes. It says here that they were using sex toys."

"Those are BDSM instruments sir," Kemi said.

"Yes. . . . Whips and dildos and collars!" He fell silent as he scanned the report again, his lips forming the words, his eyes growing bigger and bigger.

"Sarjent Limba!" He barked.

"Yes sir!" The sergeant jumped into the room.

"Do you know if Foto has finished developing the films?"

"Which one sir?"

"The photos you took at this woman's house yesterday morning, the crime scene photographs."

"I don't know, sir. We are yet to pay him, and you know how Foto gets when it comes to money." Sargent Limba was highly offended, it showed in his tone.

"We will pay him." The DPO hurriedly corrected himself. "I mean the family of the woman will pay him."

"But I have some of the pictures on my phone, if you don't mind sir,"

Sergeant Limba pulled an android phone out of his pocket, flipped through it and handed it over to his boss.

"Well done Limba, you'll go far in this profession," the DPO said as he scrolled through the pictures.

"Thank you sir." Sergeant Limba gave a smart salute.

The DPO studied the pictures on the phone as if he was preparing for his PhD thesis. He sighed regretfully at some point and returned the phone to Limba. "Thank you Sarjent, you may step out of the room now."

Limba left the office on quiet feet.

"I honestly don't know what to say," The DPO started. "Of course we've heard of cases like this. I mean there's nothing new under the sun." he tittered nervously. "Even though I don't think there are many cases like this in Nigeria, you know." He trailed off, "...or maybe the families handle it quietly." he whispered.

"Yes. We know, sir."

"She's going to be charged for manslaughter, you know?"

"Yes, sir, we do." Morieba sighed.

"Although I'm sure that there are laws on all these things in more advanced parts of the world, but this is Nigeria..." He spread his hands and got caught up studying them.

"We came to tell you one little thing sir." Kemi adopted his confidential air.

The DPO turned his attention back to the women, "Yes?"

"Tola is under psychiatric care at Yaba, and she's not been taking her meds. She has an appointment with the doctor tomorrow."

The DPO took his hands off the table and shifted his seat back. "Why didn't anybody tell me this before? You mean we've been here with a mad woman? We even locked her in a roomful of other people overnight!"

"Sir, she's not a mad woman, she suffers from depression and a medical condition called MPD, multiple-personality disorder, at least that's what it says in her file here." Kemi picked her briefcase, opened it and pulled out some files. She pushed the thickest one, with the cover falling off towards the DPO. The man shifted back again, as if touching the file might transfer 'madness' to him.

"Her doctor even wanted to come with us today," Kemi continued as she locked the briefcase. "But she had an emergency and had to return to the hospital."

Rita wondered where Kemi and Morieba got the file from. She'd never been to Yaba before, she couldn't recollect ever being there.

"Why didn't anybody tell me this? Sergeant Limba!" He barked. The policeman was back in the room with them. "This woman that you brought yesterday! Did you know she's mental?"

Sergeant Limba looked shocked, he took as many steps away from Rita as it was possible in that small room.

Rita smiled to herself.

Madness is catching, it's just like a cold, one sneeze from me and all of them will start tearing off their clothes. I wonder who's truly mad.

"This is a different case entirely!" The DPO nearly screamed.

"No it's not sir." Kemi said gently, "We know she can't be bailed and we won't want to get any civil society organization involved in this case. All we are asking for is that Tola should not be placed with other inmates, if you can find an empty cell for her... and we'll also like permission for her doctor to come and see her tomorrow — you know how these hungry human rights activists behave!"

"I've never had this kind of wahala before," the DPO stared accusingly at all the people in the room. "I don't like all these people shouting about human rights coming into my station. They never mind their own business!"

The room fell quiet as they all contemplated how irritating human rights activists could be.

"Sergeant Limba!" The DPO had started sweating profusely.

"Yes sir!"

"Can you make arrangements for an empty cell?"

"...And if a small mattress can be arranged for her, we'll really appreciate it." Morieba added sweetly.

"Mattress?" The word was a question thrown at Sergeant Limba.

"I'll see what I can do sir!"

"Clean mattress." Kemi shouted after Sergeant Limba's retreating back. The DPO turned his attention back to the women. "One more thing, your sister has refused to give her statement." He dared a look at Rita, she glared at him, he hurriedly removed his eyes from her face.

Kemi and Morieba turned accusing faces towards her.

"I'm ready to give my statement now." Rita said clearly. "It is mine, the statement is mine, but I'll give it to him if he wants."

Rita knew the room was listening to her. She didn't want to say those words, they just came out of her mouth, those were not her words. She didn't like the way they sounded.

"Good, good." The DPO shuffled the papers on his desk. "I will tell the Sergeant to take down your statement before you're removed to your cell. I don't even know if mental people can give statements. All these evil spirits running around my station now ehn? We have to do special prayer." He looked up. "Madam you will have to pay a pastor to do it."

"It's alright sir." Kemi raised placating hands. "We are ready to do anything to make her stay here comfortable."

The DPO gave Rita another nervous look. "I'm sorry you won't be able to give her any medicine while she's under arrest, but her doctor can see her tomorrow, under supervision of course."

"You're very kind sir, and your kindness will be repaid tenfold." Morieba murmured.

I just want some vodka.

"Me too my darling, I will like to drink some with you." Èsù said as Rita brushed past by them on the narrow passageway. Rita looked at them and smiled, they smiled back.

fucking little liar

Moremi, Morieba and Kudirat were in the sitting room of the mini flat at the basement of the house. They were waiting for Ortega.

Morieba was not too enamoured of the idea, but she had rejected so many other plans the girls had gone ahead and invited Ortega in spite of her protestations, that they were too young, that their ideas were too far out, and because Ortega was a thug who had once hired

lakiriboto chronicles

parents for Kudirat didn't mean he was good enough to handle the case.

"Ah but Aunty Morieba, it's only a thief that can track the footsteps of another thief at a garbage dump." Kudirat had said.

According to Ngozi, who had been delegated to investigate him, Ortega was presently the right-hand man of the president of National Union of Road Transport Workers.

"This doesn't mean he's knowledgeable about the workings of the underworld." Morieba had insisted.

But things had changed, the SMS that had landed in her phone the previous evening had her hands tied.

"Is your friend still coming or not?" Morieba had been antsy since they arrived at the flat about five minutes earlier.

"He should be here anytime soon," Moremi's tone was placatory. "He called me when he got to the toll gate."

"That boy might not come." She insisted, "I told you he's not a real criminal."

"How many criminals do you know Aunty M?" Kudirat teased her.

"I know Olori Ebi and now I know Chinwe and the people who have joined the 'blackmail of Morieba Alagbado to an inch of her life' gang, and I think you, Kudirat, have the makings of a criminal."

"That was a low one Aunty M," Kudirat said in mock annoyance.

Moremi's phone rang, "Hello. Ortega? Yes, the one with the black gate? That's our house! Tell Mallam Sule your name. We already told him you're coming, he'll bring you here."

The three women fell silent as they waited for his arrival. Kudirat jumped out of her chair and went to get the door as soon as the bell to the flat rang.

"Hi Ortega." She pulled the door open, "Mallam Sule, thanks, you may return to the gate now."

Ortega had changed in the last one and a half years. He had grown taller and filled out. His once thin and gangly body was muscular, he wore an air of confidence that had not been there when they had still been together at Bariga Comprehensive High School.

He was dressed in a pair of jeans and t-shirt, high tops graced his feet, a laptop bag was slung across his shoulder. He looked prosperous.

"It's so good to see you." Moremi found to her surprise that she meant every word.

"And you too! Hey . . . you girls are all grown up!" He said as he hugged her.

"So are you." Moremi dragged him towards Morieba. "This is our aunt, Morieba Alagbado."

"Pleasure meeting you, ma'am." Ortega shook the hand that was held out to her.

After they'd settled down, Moremi turned to Ortega.

"Would you like something to eat?"

"No, I'm alright," He protested.

"I'll get you something to drink while the girls fill you in." She hurried out of the room.

The girls understood how awkward their aunt would feel discussing what they'd come to term 'the situation', with a stranger.

"I heard what happened to Tola and her husband, that was some crazy shit man." Ortega said after a while.

Moremi didn't want to talk about Tola. She was still trying to sort out her feelings about the murder. "But not half as crazy as the story I'm about to share with you."

Kudirat handed him the folder. He pulled out the first picture and then took the others out one after the other. He examined the pictures closely. Moremi scrutinized his face just as closely, his expression of mild interest did not change. When he was done he replaced the pictures in the envelope and leaned back into the chair.

"Somebody is blackmailing our aunt." Moremi moved to the edge of her seat so he would understand the urgency of the situation. "This same person is also in possession of some documents belonging to me."

She then told him about the Will, Olori-Ebi and Morieba.

"The other girl in the pictures, that one with her back to the camera, tell me about her." He said when she was done talking,

"Chinwe Orlu," Kudirat responded, she glanced at Moremi. "We really don't know her very well, she was Aunty M's friend. We suspect she's the one that took the pictures. She disappeared just before Olori Ebi came to blackmail Aunty M."

lakiriboto chronicles

"Where were the pictures taken?"
"I really don't know, we can ask Aunty M, and she's back."
Kudirat went to pull open the door, admitting Morieba and one of the maids who was carrying a tray of drinks.
"Please help yourself." Morieba said as the maid set the drinks down on a stool in front of him.
"I'll have some water ma'am." Ortega flashed Morieba such a charming smile that she beamed back at him.
"I have a few questions concerning the pictures ma'am." His voice was cool and polite. "Where did you meet the lady in the pictures? Do you have any idea where and when they were taken?"
"Aren't you too young to be in this line of business?" Morieba blurted out.
Moremi held her breath, waiting for some nasty remark from Ortega, but he smiled instead.
"If you don't want to work with me on account of my age Ms Alagbado, I'll totally understand, but I can assure you that I'm damn good at what I do."
He rose from his seat. "Kudirat, Moremi, please do keep in touch."
"Wait! Stop!" Morieba was out of her seat too.
"You have nothing to worry about ma'am, everything that has happened so far in this flat stays here." He gave her a reassuring smile.
"No it's not that." Morieba said sheepishly, "I was out of line."
She stood toe to toe with him and looked into his eyes for a few seconds, whatever she was looking for, she found it and stepped back. "I'm sorry, I will answer your questions."
Ortega shrugged and resumed his seat.
"I met Chinwe at the mall, the one in Dugbe. I had dashed in to pick a couple of things for some friends. I was in such a hurry that I bumped into her as I exited the supermarket, spilling all her belongings. I was shocked when she burst into tears. She looked so helpless, so vulnerable, standing there in her loafers and glasses that after I helped her to pick up her things I offered to buy her a drink.
We ended up doing lunch and that was when she told me this long story about how she was a youth corper and that it was her first time

in Ibadan. She said the government hadn't paid their allowance but her flatmates had thrown her things out.

You should have seen her looking brave and sad at the same time. I didn't know when I offered her a place in my house." She paused. "It wasn't all innocent really. I was attracted to her from the get go."

Her gaze was averted.

Moremi wondered, again, why she was so ashamed, what she'd done wrong.

"I honestly didn't make the first move, she did." Morieba's voice had deepened, "I wouldn't want to take advantage of someone who's so vulnerable. She was the one that came knocking on my door in her transparent nightgown telling me about having a nightmare. I suspected that she wanted more than comforting, my instincts were screaming no. But I was attracted to her, and it is so hard for LGBT people in the country to find love..." Morieba trailed off.

Moremi could see the sadness she was struggling to hide. It was at that moment that she realised how difficult her aunt's life must have been, Morieba was so obviously different.

"I allowed her to make all the moves. That girl was good! I mean she was a good actress," she added hurriedly.

When Kudirat did not crack a smile, Moremi swallowed hers.

"She never accepted any money or gifts from me. She would buy me little things, the dark chocolate I love so much, she would bring me wine, the type, that I used to drink before I got rich enough to afford good ones. I honestly thought she loved me.

"And we only made love. I mean we only had sex in my bedroom. We couldn't risk even looking at each other intimately outside of my bedroom door!" she laughed ruefully.

"The fucking little liar."

"Did you ever meet any of her friends?" Ortega asked as he pulled a small Nokia phone out of his pocket, it was one of those old types without internet connectivity.

"No, she never brought anybody home. She usually left early for the school where she claimed she'd been posted, and returned around 2 p.m. She appeared shy, bookish . . . until that day in my bedroom." Morieba sighed into silence.

"That's not all Ortega," Moremi said, "Aunty Morieba got a text message yesterday, and that's why you're actually here."

Morieba flipped through her set and handed it to Ortega.

Yu hav noting to fear from yr uncle. He can't use computa. He hav one copy of the pix. I hav e-copies of pix & video. They are save for now. Await fourda instructions.

"Bad grammar," Ortega said after reading through the text. He returned the phone to Morieba. "Very unprofessional. I mean, it works for internet scams, but not blackmail gigs."

Moremi smirked.

"We suspect that Chinwe sent it." Kudirat tried to inject seriousness back into the conversation.

"Let me get this straight. There are two sets of people blackmailing you," he looked at Morieba, she nodded. "The first person is a family member and he's in possession of some documents belonging to Moremi,"

He turned towards Moremi. "Yes, he's blackmailing Aunty M because she's my legal guardian."

"Ah, I see. Anyway, so the guy who got the contract to do the filming is in turn blackmailing your aunt."

"Yes, we didn't even know about them until yesterday." Morieba said, "Olori Ebi is such a dunce, I mean really? You contact criminals to get you pictures that you will use to blackmail me and it didn't even occur to you that they might start blackmailing me too?"

"Maybe he just doesn't care." Moremi sighed.

Morieba shook her head, "No. He's just plain ignorant. In his stupid little mind, he probably trusts these people. He's one of those people who believe in the lie that there's honour amongst thieves. I mean he expected that I won't tell you he's blackmailing me! The way his mind works. It defies logic."

Ortega picked up his phone and dialled a number. As the phone started ringing he switched on the speaker.

"Ortega how you dey now?" A gravelly voice came over the phone.

"My chair," Ortega responded, grinning widely.

"You don reach Ibadan?"

"Yes my Chair. Baba Fryo, you're on speakerphone. I'm with a couple of pretty cool chicks I was in school with, and they need our help." He smiled up at the girls, "Moremi, Kudirat, say hello to Baba Fryo." The girls shouted their hellos.

"The girls need me to do some work for them, so I'll be needing a contact person here in Ibadan."

"That's no big deal," Baba Fryo said, "The go-to man is Sule Alapawura. I'll send you his number and tell him you're coming to see him. Don't go to him with empty mouth."

"No lele, thanks so much my chair." Ortega said.

"You're a good son to me," Baba Fryo said matter of factly and ended the call.

He looked up at the girls who were staring at him wide-eyed. "That's my chairman, he's a very nice man, you heard him?"

He had barely finished talking when his phone beeped.

"Ah, here's the number, do you girls know Sule?" He asked as he fiddled with the phone.

"Nope," Moremi looked at Kudirat in askance, she shrugged.

"I don't know him personally," Morieba cleared her throat, "but I've heard about him around town, that guy is dangerous." She smiled grimly. "I heard he's the kingpin of Alabere."

Ortega was making another call.

"Good afternoon sir, my name is Ortega. My chair, Baba Fryo said I should call you. Yes sir, we've come to do some business in your town, sir. Alright sir. I'll find you. Yes sir, I'll call you when I get there and yes, I'll bring the consultation fee, thank you sir."

"That was quick," Morieba was rather impressed. The truth was that calling Ortega had been a desperate move on their part, not in their wildest imaginings had he been this powerful in criminal circles.

"We told you Ortega is our man." Moremi and Kudirat grinned at Morieba.

"Sule said we should see him around 6 p.m." Ortega scrutinized Moremi and grinned. "I think Moremi should come along with me, if I'd known it was this kind of deal I would have brought one of my boys. You do have a baseball cap?" The last question was tossed carelessly at Moremi who grinned back at Ortega and nodded.

"It's just 4 p.m. now, I think we can have some lunch," Morieba said.
"Before we have lunch ma'am, may I ask about your budget?" Ortega's voice was all business.
"I'll deposit a million naira into your account," Morieba sounded a little anxious, "Would that be enough?"
Ortega smiled, "One million should do, for now... One more thing, ma'am, I'll need to stay around till this business is over and maybe get one or two boys in with me. We'll need to beef up your security and sweep your house for hidden cameras."
A panicked look flashed across Morieba's face.
"No, please, don't." She shook her head, "I've spent most of my life trying not to become a prisoner to my wealth..."
Ortega smiled reassuringly, "Madam, you won't even notice they are there, it's for your safety. We are not going to do anything heavy..."
Morieba was thinking furiously, "You know what? Let's sort this business out first, then we can discuss the least intrusive options for our protection."
"Sounds good."
Morieba's phone rang, she looked at the caller ID and sighed, "sorry I have to take this call." She made her way out of the flat, when she reached the doorway she faced Ortega, "by the way you can make use of this flat for as long as you want, your boys are welcome too. Just don't throw any wild parties."
"Don't worry ma'am. The partying will come after we've completed the job." Ortega grinned.

the money making machine

"Catch!" Olori Ebi tossed a black polythene bag at Amope. She stretched out one arm, missed it, and then got on her hands and knees to trawl for it on the floor. His expression was a mixture of pity and disgust as he stared at her.
Amope was all skin and bones, her head close shaven. Her dark skin had a grey tinge to it, and there were dark spots all over her thin

arms. Her face though, her face was still smooth, with intelligent eyes that had seen everything. Thick, curvy lips and an aristocratic nose that turned up at the tip.

I, Aduke Olatorera Alagbado, being of sound mind and body to my only daughter Amope Omobolanl Alagbado, I bequeath all my worldly goods which would be administered by her until her daughter, my granddaughter, Moremi Asake Alagbado, turns 21.

Underlisted are the aforementioned properties:

1. A three storey building at 28, Moruwa close, Lekki, Ajah Roundabout, Lagos.
2. Three semi-detached houses: Nos 4, 5 and 6, Awosika Avenue, Old Bodija, Ibadan.
3. Two semi-detached, Nos 34A/34B, Moroway Drive, Ikoyi.
4. One bungalow, SW8/166/897 Idi-Ikan, Ibadan.

Amope whimpered as she drew the small sachet containing the brown sugar out of the bag, she rubbed it against her cheek and smiled blissfully. Her eyes lit up like those of a child who'd just been handed a bag of sweet.

The elders have a saying that once you own a slave, you own all their earthly possessions. Not that I'm saying that Amope is my slave.

"Thank you my dear, darling, uncle." She sat on the bare mattress, tightened the ankara wrapper around her chest and dragged a small leather bag from one corner of the room.

The room itself was a tiny, square shaped thing that had been a store-room in its former life. Olori Ebi had placed her there because he didn't want her in the main house. Junkies would steal and sell anything they lay their hands on when the biting need for a high hits them, he didn't want to wake up to an empty house.

The room was sandwiched between the main house and the outdoor toilet. He thought it apt, since she could no longer be considered human, only human beings were allowed to live in a house. Amope belonged to a new species created from heroin. She was a zombie, a half-dead thing well on her way to being flushed down the toilet.

"Amope, Amope, Amope, how many times did I call you?"

"Three times my darling uncle." She looked at him with eyes snapping with impatience, but Olori Ebi forged on.

"Remember our deal that you will clean up in preparation for our return to the bank the week after next."

...however, this will only be in effect if the said sole heir has been declared drug free by independent doctors from Union Bank, Zenith Bank and High Street Bank.

"Don't worry uncle, I got this." She sniffled as she laid her tools of trade neatly, reverently, on the stool in front of her; a syringe, a lighter, a candle, a spoon and a long rag. "Like I told you yesterday, I'm not feeling too hot, and I only need to eat very well, lost my appetite, but I'll be fine."

"Isn't that what you said last week? This is getting too long. I really can't afford to keep supplying you if you won't help me."

She paused and looked at him with eyes brimming with tears, "Please uncle, don't do this. You know I'm a very sick woman, you know this!"

"I'm sorry mai dia." Olori Ebi touched her shoulder with the tip of his fingers. "It's not that I don't understand. All you need is to be clean for a week, then we'll go for the test, after that you can continue..." he pointed at the sachet she was still holding.

She wiped a line of tears that was snaking its way from her eye to her cheek, sniffled and continued with what she was doing.

As she measured the sugar brown heroin carefully onto a strip of paper, she paused and looked up at Olori Ebi, who was still standing by the doorway, her face a big question mark. "May I have some privacy please?"

Olori Ebi opened his mouth in surprise. He clapped his hands and was about to say something derisive when he caught the steely look on her face.

He swallowed his words and stepped out of the room, shutting the door quietly behind him.

"Ah!" He ejaculated as he made for the main house, "So beggars are choosers! See this small girl ordering me around."

He tried to remember the last time someone had spoken to him in that tone of voice but failed. Morieba didn't count, she was an ill-mannered girl, and rudeness was the trade-in-mark of children who hadn't been raised properly.

"Because I want to eat beef, I am now forced to call a cow my elder brother. A junkie! A mere beggarly prostitute telling me to give her some privacy in my own house! Why am I even surprised?" He fumed as he stepped into the main house. "She is her mother's daughter after all, a useless bunch of women."

He suddenly remembered seeing L'Egba snooping around his house the other day. The front door had been ajar and she had emerged from the direction of the backyard claiming that she was looking for Iyawo.

How had that snoopy woman learnt that Amope is with me?

"Baami the car is ready." Lekan was standing right in his path, he was beaming.

Olori Ebi glared at his son with ill-concealed annoyance. The boy had been on at him about one of his 'friends' who had a 'deal' that only came 'once in a lifetime'. But Olori Ebi knew his son, he was thicker than two bricks. Although strangers could be fooled into thinking he was smart, because of his good looks and bulging muscles which made him appear like he spent a lot of time in the gym. But the klutz was too lazy to do anything as strenuous as exercise. He spent his days mooning after women and his nights drinking anything that came in dense coloured bottles.

If it had been Quadri that brought the deal he wouldn't have been so leery, but this was Lekan! The same boy that brought home a girl who looked like the parody of a sophisticate with an inch thick pancake on her face, blood red lipstick, blue eye-pencil and kohl lined lower lids, which didn't piss Olori-Ebi off as much as when he had introduced the girl to him as his fiancée.

He had decided to indulge him, not because he was interested in a 'Hausa Prince with more money than sense', but he wanted to prove to Lekan, once and for all, that he was a fool, and maybe prevent him from bringing more lame ideas.

Olori Ebi listened to his prattle, about money making machines, and shady deals by the government, all the way to the office. He had been involved in too many scams not to recognize something that smelt like it.

So when a young man, with regal features and milky white skin walked into his office, he was ill-prepared and rather taken aback.

"Baami, this is the Mahmoud I told you about." Lekan's grin split his face into two.

"Please, please, sit down," Olori Ebi's heart started beating in a manner that was totally alien to him. If anybody had bothered to ask if he had a heart, he would have told them that he had none, but there it was, fluttering around his chest like a demented winged thing.

"No, no, please don't sit there," He stuttered as the young man made to sit on a broken chair. "Lekan! Go to the secretary's office and bring your... our visitor a proper chair befitting a man of his status."

"I won't like to put you to any trouble sir."

His well cultured voice made Olori Ebi's hands tremble. He knew people like the young man smiling at him with pearly white teeth, he'd heard them speak before, he'd even been in the company of men that spoke like good breeding was dropping off their lips, but none had ever directed their words at him. For the first time in his life, he was conscious of his lack of sophistication and education. He cleared his throat and mimicked the well-rounded vowels that had just caressed his ears.

"It's no trouble."

Lekan was back in the room with a proper chair. He noticed how grimy it looked and cringed. He suddenly realized that he hadn't painted his office in the past two years. A ratty window blind was fluttering behind him, a 2008 calendar was off to his right.

Haba Raufu get a grip!

The young man sat down immediately after the broken chair had been replaced.

"I'm sure Lekan has told you about the deal," the young man launched into the business without further ado, a boy after my heart. Olori Ebi leaned towards him with rapt attention, his arms resting on the table.

"It's quite simple sir," he drew a card out of his pocket and pushed it across the table with his long fingers. Olori Ebi picked it up and pretended to read it.

"I'm Mahmoud Abubk'r ibn Traore. I work with the CBN as a store manager." He pulled a phone out of his pocket, fiddled with it and gave it to Olori Ebi. Lekan hurried to his father's side and showed him pictures of the president shaking Mahmoud's hand, he and the CBN governor at what seemed like a party, and finally some chunky machines, the likes of which Olori Ebi had never seen before.

"The party in power is preparing for next elections, and you know very well that this costs a lot of money. Last year the government decided to change Nigeria's currency notes and bought the machines that you've just seen on my phone, but when they realised that the cost of production might be too risky in Nigeria, they changed their minds and decided to print the new currencies in SA."

Olori Ebi wondered where SA was, but he nodded in agreement, far be it for him to behave like a bush-man in the presence of this …this prince… the cream du la cream, high class, English speaking young man.

"We are looking for trustworthy individuals that can handle this deal for us."

He asked the only disquieting question on his mind, "Why me?"

"Luck sir! Whichever god you worship is obviously on your side." Mahmoud gave a slow smile. "I met Lekan at a party thrown for me by my cousin and we hit it off immediately, seeing how street smart he is I told him about this deal and he said you were an ideal candidate."

Olori Ebi looked at Lekan with dawning respect.

"You are well known in this community." Mahmoud's voice was still caressing his ears, the same way that drink what's it called 'Irish Pomade'? no Irish Cream! — caressed your throat.

"And all the people we have spoken to assured us that you are a discreet and trustworthy person."

On seeing the skeptical look in Olori Ebi's eyes, he raised his hands in defeat. "Alright, not everybody had good things to say about you, but the few that did had good points. And we carried out a thorough investigation sir. Permit me to say that we know that you're one of the founding fathers of Alabere."

"What are you accusing me of?" Olori Ebi glared at him.

"We are not accusing you of anything sir, please hear me out." He waited for Olori Ebi's nod before continuing. "We know you are one of the founding fathers of Alabere, and we also know you left the place and had become a businessman, a honest one living off the rents of your properties and managing your family's lands."

Olori Ebi did not allow him to see how pleased he had been by that remark.

"You were chosen for your ruggedness and determination. We also know that with your background this kind of deal won't be strange. The fact that you do not have any political affiliations also weighs heavily in your favour."

Olori Ebi stared at the young man for the longest time. He weighed his words, his options. This might be the deal that would seal off, once and for all, his claim on Alhaja's property, he needed to convert all of them into cash ASAP, and he also needed a source of income, an investment that would rival the ones Morieba constantly boasted about. The money making machine was sounded pretty attractive.

Everybody knew that politicians were a bunch of crooks, if not for Alabere, he would have been a big man now... kai!

"There's really nothing more to say sir. I'll give you time to decide whether you're in or not." Mahmoud drew an envelope out of his pocket and gave it to Olori Ebi. "I'll give you a week to check out my background sir. Here are my details. You also have to understand that this is a secret, you'll have to be discreet."

"You don't need to tell me that," Olori Ebi bristled. Mahmoud's face was expressionless.

"If I don't hear back from you by the end of the week, I'll know you're not interested." He rose from his seat and extended a hand across the table. "Have a good day sir."

He was nearly at the door when Olori Ebi remembered something, "Wait, you didn't tell me how much this would cost me."

"Oh, I'm so sorry." Mahmoud fished a card out of his pocket and pushed it across the table.

"Alright sir, I hope to hear back from you soon. Lekan, please see me off."

Olori Ebi took a good look at the numbers boldly printed on the card, it was 80 million, naira. That was when it finally sank in that Mahmoud wasn't joking.

He fished out his phone from the voluminous fold of his agbada and placed a call to Sule Alapawura – *he uses computers, he would know what to do.*

yaba left

Kudirat wanted to weep as she watched Tola being dragged forcefully from behind the counter by three burly policemen.

"There is really no need for this violence!" Morieba shouted as she and Kemi ran towards the men. Another police officer blocked their path.

All the female officers were gathered near the doorway, craning their necks to watch the spectacle and discuss in loud voices how they suspected all along that 'the woman was crazy', because no woman in her right mind would ever 'kill her own husband.' They discussed the hands of witches and wizards that must be in IT, and then went on to share their experiences of 'women who ran naked in the streets without any prior notice.'

Kudirat blocked out their chatter and moved away from them.

Morieba and Kemi were begging the officer barring their way. "Madam, we will handle this! She is a criminal. All these acting doesn't do anything for her case! If anything she's just giving us more evidence!"

But Kudirat was more concerned about Tola.

"Leave me alone! Tell these people to leave me alone!" The eerie thing was that she wasn't raving, she wasn't shouting, her voice was even, she was making a statement of fact. "You think I can't fight you all off with just one finger? I'm just feeling sorry for you."

She wondered how Tola was able to maintain that tone of voice all the while struggling with the men. As a policeman holding a chain tried to wrap it around Tola's ankle, a well-aimed kick caught him on the chin. Kudirat winced as he fell down.

She wondered where Tola got her strength. Her arms were already cuffed behind her back, but that apparently hadn't any effect on her. She jerked, she kicked, she heaved like a volcano that was about to erupt into a fountain of hot lava.

Kudirat didn't know that tears were pouring down her face until she felt saltiness on her tongue. She used the edge of her t-shirt to wipe off her face. A policeman came from the direction of the passageway and tried to grab Tola by the throat.

Kudirat decided she would no longer watch. The last thing she saw before running out of the station was Tola hitting her head on the edge of the counter as she struggled to evade the chokehold.

She ran out of the police station, through the gate towards the car that had brought her in from Ibadan that morning and found to her dismay that it had been locked. She considered returning to the station and collecting the key from Morieba but changed her mind. She didn't want to experience any more pain.

Across the road, just in front of the police station fence, was a woman selling sweets and kolanuts. The bench the woman was seated on was long, longer than the small tray of goods she monitored as seriously as the women selling gold in Balogun market kept an eye on their goods. Kudirat crossed to her side of the road, smiled at the woman and bought some Tom-Tom sweets.

"Please ma, may I sit down beside you?"

The woman gave her a vaguely suspicious look but nodded in assent. She sat down and unwrapped the sweet, but she didn't put it in her mouth. She couldn't. Tola's image filled her head.

The hair that stuck out in weedlike clumps all over her head. The wild look in her eyes, blood spurting out of her head as she hit it on the edge of the slab.

Why did the police have to be so violent? How did she get to this point? What happened to the woman that I used to know? Yes she hadn't been totally sane but this Tola is so different from the woman I lived with for several years.

Kudirat and Moremi had debated the issue of Tola killing her husband. Both of them held long discussions about Wale, they talked about how wicked he had been. How he had abused them physically and psychologically, how he had sexually molested them. They had finally talked about Jesulayomi, the day she'd come to tell them about how her dad would kiss her and touch her whenever she was in bed. They talked about Tola's depression, but neither of them had ever envisaged this violent end to a relationship that shouldn't have been.

Kudirat swore that no man would ever put her in such a position, she wondered why Tola hadn't left, why her parents had not taken her to see a doctor. She thought about how love drove women to madness.

She recalled her own mother, the shady circumstances surrounding her marriage to her father, the painful whispers of the villagers that time and distance hadn't alleviated. She thought about how easily her mother had given her up.

Why do women never stand up for themselves? Why do they always allow themselves to become victims?

"Kudirat!" Morieba's voice jerked her out of her thoughts. "Where are you?"

"I'm here Aunty M." She rose from the chair and crossed the road.

"Get into the car." Morieba ordered gruffly. She inserted a key into the ignition, but instead of starting the car she put her head on the wheel and started hyperventilating.

Kudirat didn't know what to do, so she caressed Morieba's back.

As an ambulance drove out of the grounds of the police station, its siren wailing like the lost soul it was bearing, Morieba sat up straight and dashed tears off her face.

She started the engine and drove off the premises. She followed the ambulance as closely as she possibly could, in the slow moving traffic heading out of Bariga towards Yaba.

"Where's aunty Kemi?" Kudirat asked as the silence in the car stretched out.

"She's in the ambulance with Tola and the doctor."

"Is Aunty Tola alright now?"

"I don't know about her being alright, but she's certainly calmer, the

lakiriboto chronicles

doctor gave her an injection, she says it would calm her down till we get to the hospital. But why?" She shouted and hit the steering wheel with her palm.

"Why what, aunty?"

"Why didn't that bastard DPO call us early enough?" A groove formed between her eyes, "We've already told you that Tola was sick, we told you the very week she was brought into your station!? You knew that this woman hadn't been sleeping or eating any of the food we've been bringing to her. You knew that she's been talking to herself. Even the most idiotic person knows when someone is having a manic episode. Instead of calling us, or her doctor, you kept her locked up, claiming that you thought we made up the story of her mental illness so as to keep her out of prison! What nonsense! What other proof does that bastard need? What if she'd harmed herself? If Kemi hadn't gone there yesterday and insisted she must see her sister the girl could have died!"

Kudirat was not used to listening, but she swallowed her words as torrents of anger and frustration flowed out of Morieba's lips.

"See why I did not want to involve the police in my own case? Isn't it the same useless way they would have handled it? My goodness! People are so incompetent. So lacking in empathy and kindness! Even if she's lying, shouldn't you have called a doctor to come and verify? Is he a doctor? Does he know anything about psychiatry?"

They were soon caught in a hold up and Morieba slowed the car to a crawl.

The ambulance was still wailing, ineffectively, because there was no room for manoeuvring. She fell quiet.

"Everything is going to be alright aunty," Kudirat said, "You'll see, we'll all be fine."

Morieba's phone started ringing.

"Pick that call and tell whoever that I'll call them back," She inched the car forward.

Kudirat looked at the caller ID it was Moremi.

"Hello Moremi."

"What happened to your phone? I've been calling you all afternoon."

"My phone died. Aunty M and I are stuck in traffic, she said she'll call you back."
"I wasn't calling to talk to her. I just want to find out how you guys are doing and how is Aunty Tola? What happened, why did Aunty Kemi insist that Aunty M should come to Lagos?"
Kudirat sighed. "It's a long story, you'll have to wait till we return to Ibadan to hear the full gist. We are on our way to Yaba right now."
"It's alright, hope you guys will make it home today."
"I doubt if that will happen." Kudirat wanted to say a lot of things. She wanted to describe the things she'd seen at the police station, how she was suddenly scared of the kind of shit love could cause. But she didn't because she knew this wasn't the right time or place.
"By the way, tell Aunty M that Ortega has found the woman that carried out the setup, we are going to see Sule Alapawura later today."
"Oh great!" Kudirat tried to sound enthusiastic, but Ibadan and its own set of anxieties seemed so far away that she really didn't care.
Moremi must have sensed her disinterest. "Guess what? Call me whenever you finally get to charge your phone."
"Alright, Moremi, we've just driven into the grounds of Yaba Psychiatric Hospital, I'll talk to you later."
Kudirat ended the call just as Morieba found a space to park the car. By the time they walked back to the where the ambulance was parked Tola had been strapped down to a gurney, she was fast asleep.
The three policemen, who had been struggling with Tola joined them by the ambulance. Kudirat noted that they had guns slung on their shoulders. The DPO was there too, his rounded head trying to outshine the sun, he looked embarrassed. Morieba went to stand beside Kemi.
"They are going to book her in now. I'm so sorry for dragging you all the way down from Ibadan, I was at my wit's end. I've been going to the police headquarters and the court to get this case fast tracked but, you know how frustrating those processes can be. Something just told me to go and see her yesterday.
That lovely girl, Ngozi, is the one that has been helping me to deliver

lakiriboto chronicles

food to her, so when I asked if she'd seen Tola at all, the girl said the policemen only made her eat out of the food and then collected it from her and delivered it to Tola by themselves, which is the normal procedure. Alarm bells went off in my head when she complained that they hadn't been returning the food flasks to her. I was even thinking that they were eating all the food and starving Tola not knowing that it was way worse.

When I got to the station yesterday that useless DPO, who has been collecting money from me refused to let me see her! That was when I started pressing buttons. One of my friends who knew a top official was the one that finally called the DPO. They couldn't even bring her out, she was really in a state.

One of the policemen confessed to me that everybody in the station had been aware of the fact that Tola hadn't slept in close to two weeks. But when they had reported it to the DPO he'd dismissed it claiming that's how women are always forming mental."

The gurney was pushed towards the Emergency Section. Kudirat fell behind the women and for the first time in her entire life, she didn't feel like eavesdropping on a conversation. She walked as far away as possible not to overhear them, but near enough not to lose them in the crowd of patients, family members and medical personnel that filled the emergency room of Yaba Psychiatric Hospital also known as Yaba Left.

asas motel near molete bridge

Moremi stared at her reflection in the mirror and decided she might just get used to her new look. Her formerly wild curls had been dyed black, and dreadlocked. She was wearing contact lenses that changed her green eyes into brown. She pulled a face-cap over her head and straightened her t-shirt before finally turning away from the mirror. She picked a knapsack from the foot of the bed and descended the staircase.

Kudirat, Ortega and Morieba were seated on the patio, round a table, their heads lowered towards a laptop on the table.

"I'm ready," she announced as she bounced through the sitting room towards them. "What are you doing?"

"Uploading your article about the Emir of Daura," Ortega said as he clicked a button, uploading the picture and a write up to one of the many blogs they'd created since they started the campaign over a month ago.

The picture was that of a middle-aged man wearing yards and yards of Babariga and a headgear that rivalled that of the Emir of Kano, he was sitting astride a horse, a horde of people surrounded him, their hands were in the air. Another picture showed him alighting from a Rolls-Royce.

The headline read, Unveiled: The Emir of Daura, the 50th richest man in the world is a Nigerian!

"Have you seen Mukhtar?" He asked as he rose from the spindly legged chair he'd been seated on.

"No, I've not even seen him today." Moremi shrugged.

Mukhtar was one of the laziest people Moremi had ever encountered. He was either slouching about the flat or sleeping. But she'd seen him in action and totally understood why Ortega would work with him. He was a chameleon who could switch from one character to another within the twinkling of an eye. One moment he was speaking Hausa inflected Queen's English, the next he was a pidgin speaking thug from the streets of Warri.

"If we get downstairs and he's not there..."

Ortega allowed his words to hang in the air. He tapped Kudirat on the shoulder. "Once it finishes uploading please share it on the other platforms. Don't forget to tag Moremi and Mukhtar so they can share it on their platforms too. Hopefully a couple of other bloggers will steal it before tonight."

"Aye, aye captain." Kudirat retorted.

Morieba looked drained, she had lost a lot of weight and had taken to lurking indoors. She was to be constantly found with her phone google searching her name. She'd gotten worse in the past week when a girl's badly shot lesbian video had been uploaded on the internet and the homophobes had come out in droves, howling for her death.

As if that wasn't bad enough, after a few more threatening notes, they'd finally received the 'fourda instrutions' from the blackmailers. Cum to asas motel near Molete birge 6pm on d dot with 4 million Naira in raw cash. Put d moni inside Ghana mus go. Wait fourda instructions. Wear red cloth.

Moremi never found out what Ortega would have done to Mukhtar because they met him leaning against the Volkswagen bug that Morieba had given to them to move around with. He was smoking a spliff. He used his fingers to put out the light and placed the roach inside a cigarette box.

Ortega pulled open the door and folded the driver's seat. It took three of them some time to manoeuvre the huge bag into the car.

Ortega pulled a tracker, the shape and size of a matchbox out of his pocket, activated it and inserted it as deeply as it was possible into the bag. He zipped it up. Mukhtar jumped in beside the bag while Ortega and Moremi sat in front.

As Moremi drove through the gate, Ortega dialled a number, "Oga Chuks, yes we're on our way... alright then, are the boys in position? Great! Don't worry I go settle all of you nah. Yes I still have your account numbers. I've told you that you'll get the money as soon as we've done the job."

They fell quiet as Moremi concentrated on navigating the usual hold up at the Challenge roundabout.

Ortega alighted in front of St. Anne's Grammar School. Moremi drove further down, pulled up in front of Asas Hotel, alighted from the car and waited for the call.

Her phone beeped. She fished it out of her pocket and read the text message out loud to Mukhtar who had just lit up the roach again and was studying the men furtively entering and coming out of the whorehouse.

Carry Ghana-mus- go... be working down to the birge.

Moremi forwarded the text message to Ortega as she and Mukhtar pulled the heavy bag out of the car. She locked the car door and went to help Mukhtar with the bag. They lifted the bag with both hands and hobbled down the road as if their legs were tied together. Moremi wondered just how the blackmailers intended to carry all that money off.

Ortega had made fun of what he called their stone-age methods. "If I were doing this kind of deal, I'll open a false account, have you guys transfer the money to me and clear it out immediately. E-banking has made all these things less messy. These guys have a basic knowledge of how all these things work. They are smart, but not as smart as they imagine."

As Moremi and Mukhtar drew closer to the underside of the bridge a young man dashed past them followed by a crowd of people shouting Ole! Thief! Stop him! They were still trying to find their way out of the press when a heavy chested man grabbed the heavy bag from them as if it was feather and tossed it backwards. The bag was caught by another pair of hands, mid-air, and that was the last Moremi saw of it.

She turned to say something to Mukhtar but he had been swallowed by the crowd that seemed to have increased, the man that took the bag from her had melted into the melee. Moremi decided to stop struggling as she was borne along like a piece of debris by the tidal wave of human bodies chasing after a thief, after themselves, they were chasing after a specter.

By the time she was deposited near the motel the crowd had melted into the night. She was dialling Ortega's number when Mukhtar, looking as ragged as she felt, appeared beside her. He fished a crumpled pack of cigarettes from his pocket and lit up.

"Ortega," She said as soon as the phone call was picked, "the bag was stolen from us."

"Nice operation with the crowd, didn't think they'll do something like that. But don't worry, we are still one step ahead." He sounded amused, "just click on the Tracka icon on your phone and follow the money."

Moremi handed her phone to Mukhtar and jumped into the car.

"It's not passworded." She said Mukhtar smirked. She thanked her lucky stars, as she'd been doing since the beginning of the operation, that Ortega and Mukhtar were on her side.

"I think they are headed towards a place called Oke-Ado." He said after a while, "do you know the directions or do we have to use google maps?"

Moremi flashed him a cold look because of his condescending tone, but continued driving towards Oke-Ado.

He fiddled with the sound system, Nigeria's hip-hop filled the small interior of the car. Moremi wound down the windows to let in the cold evening air, and let out their songs of war and the sweetly sick smell of maryjay.

They were soon at the night market that Oke-Ado was famous for. There were no street lights near it so it was lit with oil-lamps and lanterns. Oke-Ado was a rumoured portal between the substantial and insubstantial.

Èsù ported from the Volkswagen bug into the crowded market. "Turn left."

Moremi's phone started beeping, Mukhtar turned off the music, he switched on the speaker. "The guys are in a place called Gbadebo Street, I'm with Chuks and his boys. Park in front of the High Court and wait for me, we might not take that long, and Mukhtar, for heaven's sake don't smoke up or play loud music!"

As Moremi pulled up in front of the High Court two policemen approached them shinning the weak yellow light of their torches into the car.

"Young man!" One of the policemen leaned into the car. "Why are you parking here?"

"Ah please oga, my brother and I are waiting for our older brother who went to see one of his friends at Iyaganku Quarters, he asked us to wait here for him." Moremi deliberately lowered the pitch of her voice.

The other policeman went to the passenger's side and shone his torch on Mukhtar's face. "Are you sure this one is your brother?"

"Yes, sir." Mukhtar's voice was pure Eton with a whisper of Hausa.

"Somebody has been smoking marijuana in this car!" The policeman shone his torch deeper into the car. Moremi swore underneath her breath and restrained herself from giving Mukhtar an accusatory look. "Step out of the car, let's see you."

Mukhtar shrugged and pulled open his side of the door. He stepped out with a charming smile on his face. Moremi turned off the ignition and did the same. She couldn't summon any smile for the men.

"Driver's licence!" one of the policemen barked as he lined Mukhtar and Moremi against the car.

Moremi pulled out her wallet and handed it over to him. Ortega had arranged the license for her almost as soon as he taught her how to drive.

"Car papers!" He barked again after examining the driver's license with his torchlight. Moremi opened the car door and took the ziplock bag containing the papers out of the dashboard. The policeman was still examining the papers when another car pulled up beside them. Ortega and Chuks alighted from the car.

"Officers!" Chuks smiled at the men.

"Chuks, Chuks! So you know these boys?" They were all smiles and shaking hands.

"They are my younger ones. Did they do anything?" Chuks was all concern.

"Ah, no, we are just trying to make sure they don't do anything." The policeman with a sense of humor answered.

"They have to leave now. I'll take care of the rest."

"Mukhtar, abeg come and help me with the bags and laptops." Ortega said.

Moremi pulled open the door and folded the driver's seat so they could pile the laptop bags, and laptops without bags and charging cords and iPads and power banks and memory banks and flash drives into the car.

"Una dey sell laptop?" One of the policemen asked curiously.

"Nooo," Chuks laughed at first and then his voice turned steely. "My brother is an engineer, he's going to help me to fix them."

"Goodnight officers and thank you." Ortega said as Moremi drove off.

"So?" She asked as they emerged into Oke-Ado once again.

Èsù hopped back into the car, they stretched out their legs and watched, for that was what gods did, they watched over human beings as they unfold their own destinies.

"Nothing, really," Ortega replied in a pre-occupied manner, he had one of the laptops opened on his lap. "We followed the money to the house of one woman like that, Chuks took over from there."

"I didn't hear any shooting." Mukhtar craned his neck backwards.

"We didn't need to shoot, Chuks' boys outnumbered them, and they were taken by surprise, so they all surrendered when we said we've only come for their phones and laptops. They hadn't even opened the bag yet. It's weird, they really believe we'll just bring them a bag full of money!"

"I'd like to be there when they find out that their money is 90% paper." Mukhtar laughed.

"We can always drop you off so you'll go and find out." Ortega muttered.

Moremi couldn't laugh, she was too nervous. What if none of the computers contains the videos and pictures?

"I hope no-one is following us though," she said.

"Don't worry about that, the boys have the place on lockdown, nobody comes in, no one goes out, they'll be there for the next two hours."

They were nearly home when Ortega shouted, "Jackpot!"

Moremi was trembling as she parked the car and jumped out, Ortega was out in a flash, the laptop containing pictures and videos still opened. Mukhtar whooped.

"Kudirat! Aunty M!" Moremi shouted as she ran towards the front door, "We found the damned pictures!"

"There's still a lot to be done," Ortega said as they sat round the dining table later that night.

The girls groaned.

"We have to wipe off the memories of all the systems and clean up the memory banks too." Mukhtar said before shoving a forkful of spaghetti into his mouth.

"And then what will you do with all those devices?" Morieba asked.

"Nothing," Ortega smiled at her, "you don't want to know about this remember? By the way ma'am, have you made the calls?"

Morieba smiled, a slow, wicked turning up of her lips. "No one will give him tissue to wipe his butt."

season 7
the mugunization of olori-ebi
(2014-2015)

the best laid plans of mice o' men

Olori Ebi was in a foul mood. If anybody had told him that raising 70 million naira would be so difficult he would have thought the person was stupid. Not that he'd tried to raise that kind of money before, but a man of his social standing shouldn't experience such difficulties.

Every plan he'd made to raise the money had been torpedoed by the fools he'd surrounded himself with. Amope had been the first person to mess up his plans.

After a week of going cold turkey, which he'd ensured by locking her in the store room. He had gotten a shock at the hospital when she'd tested positive to heroin and some other substances he hadn't even known were in existence.

He hadn't even bothered to return to the bank; he dumped Amope back at his house and ordered Lekan to lock her up again.

As if that wasn't bad enough Cherie Coco had called to accuse him of setting her up. He didn't understand how she'd thought he'd been able to pull that off. The long and short of it was that they'd lost Morieba's pictures and videos to a bunch of gun-totting bastards. She claimed he did it because he didn't want to pay the balance of her money.

Lekan popped his head into the room. "Baami, Mahmoud is here, he just drove into the complex."

Olori Ebi ground the heels of his hand into his eye, an ache had started in the regions of his left eye.

"Do you want me to tell him to come back some other time?" Lekan's voice was full of sympathy. There was nothing Olori Ebi hated more than sympathy.

He straightened his spine, and in spite of his pounding eye, he yelled. "Tell him to come upstairs! In fact go and bring him for me."
Lekan hurriedly left the room, shutting the door quietly.
Olori Ebi pulled out his drawer and opened a sachet of Alabukun, he flapped the small bag, expertly tore the upper end of the sachet open and emptied its powdery content straight into his throat. The acidic powder stung, but he picked the other sachet and swallowed that one too and as expected the headache receded immediately.
By the time Lekan returned with Mahmoud, Olori Ebi felt fine, almost happy, the four shots of schnapps he downed quickly after swallowing the alabukun also helped.
"Mallam Mahmoud." He rose from his chair and smiled at the young man, who was wearing a khaki brown jalamia. He was particularly glad that his office has had a make-over since the last meeting.
The walls had been painted a deep green, the old calendar thrown out, a brilliant yellow curtain fluttered over the window.
"It's good to see you again sir." Mahmoud shook his proffered hand.
"Please sit down," He gestured to the newly upholstered chair.
Lekan fetched a bottle of water from the newly installed fridge and placed it in front of their visitor. He fussed over Mahmoud for a while before finally leaving.
"My boss, the CBN Governor, informed me that you've called to make enquiries." He opened the conversation and sipped some water.
Olori Ebi took note of the delicate way he handled the glass.
"I hope you are not offended, but you know eighty million naira is not the kind of money one wants to joke around with."
There was no need to mention that he'd gotten Sule to look the boy up on the internet too.
Sule had shown him pictures of the boy on that Facebook something and Instagram. The boy like to take picture! He is always at one party or the other! There's even one picture he took with a man Sule said was the son of the president! Ah! The boy has money and wristwatches and perfumes! Children of nowadays are not shy about showing off their wealth at all!
Olori Ebi liked the internet, he had decided to buy a laptop once this

money thing works out, he would go to the internet and look at pictures. Ah!

Mahmoud laughed. "If you hadn't done a proper background check on me, walahi, I would have thought we've come to the wrong person."

He relaxed somewhat.

"So, is the money ready?"

Olori Ebi knew the question would come, and he'd thought of several ways of holding Mahmoud off till he raised the capital. A crazy idea slipped into his mind at that moment, and for once in his life, he decided to test the waters of honesty.

"I have a problem, my friend." He started before he lost his liver. "I have not been able to raise the money."

Mahmoud picked up the glass of water and took another sip, he looked at Olori Ebi through sad eyes.

"All the people I thought could loan me the money had one excuse or the other. I even tried to borrow the money with some deeds but the amount those shylocks are offering is way too low. I suspect it's the handiwork of my enemies!" Olori Ebi leaned towards Mahmoud confidentially, "and I've been thinking that since you work in a bank, I mean the Central Bank," he lowered his head, his voice, his eyes trained on the younger man. "I was thinking that maybe you can borrow me some money."

Mahmoud made to say something but Olori Ebi raised his hand. "I am willing to part with deeds to my properties, and once this deal is done, you will have your money back within the month!"

"I'm so sorry sir." Mahmoud stood up without any more ado.

Olori Ebi's heart flew out of the door ahead of the business deal, that one deal that would have changed his life and shut up the mouths of his enemies. He nearly grabbed his head so he could give in to the tearing up of his heart, his hopes.

"I really can't help you. I have already stuck out my neck bringing an unknown person into this mix, but how do I go back and tell them that you don't even have the cash?"

He stretched out his hand and took Olori Ebi's limp one in his, patted the hand and made for the door.

Olori Ebi did not know when he let out a mewl of pain as Mahmoud's hand touched the door knob. Instead of twisting it and exiting the office, he paused.

"Wait a minute!" His eyes were smiling. "I think I have a solution to your problem."

Olori Ebi jumped out of his chair and met Mahmoud who was already halfway back into the room, he grabbed the young man's hands before he knew what he was doing and dropped them instantly.

"Do you know the Emir of Daura?"

Olori Ebi shook his head.

"He's my uncle, and sir, he's the fiftieth richest man in the whole of Africa. Do you have all the title deeds of the properties with you?"

Olori Ebi nodded mutely, he did not want to say anything to make the magic of the moment evaporate.

"Good, we'll look through the documents together and decide the ones you should give him."

Olori Ebi dashed back to his desk, bent underneath his table and grabbed out a box full of documents.

"No need for stories my dia," he said as he emerged from underneath the table, he plunked the box down with an air of satisfaction, "You can have everything."

aromental

"I'd like to talk about your parents today." The doctor announced in the voice of a teacher talking to a particularly slow student. Tola, who was seated across from him on an uncomfortable, hard backed chair, studied the table separating them - it was neat, with books piled in a clean stack on one side and files on the other, but the gulf that separated them was wider than that table.

The doctor repeated his statement; Tola finally looked at him straight in the eye, she smoothed her shapeless green dress over her hips. Not a word crossed her lips.

The doctor leaned back on his leather chair, his face carefully blank, she shifted her gaze to the pair of pink bathroom slippers on her feet. Twenty seconds into the silence and Dr Kabir changed track. "I must say that you have done very nicely since you were first brought in here. Discovering your painting skills is also helping to accelerate your recovery."

Tola didn't think Dr Kabir was good at what he does, she wondered how his forehead managed to give off such shine in the gloomy room. He was so young and arrogant. He actually believed he knew everything about the human condition, about her.

She'd been seeing him since the first day she'd been brought to the asylum and she'd not seen any improvement in his methods.

"I hardly have any education," she ruminated out loud as she fished a pack of cigarettes from her pocket. "The only thing I've done well is to give birth to three children, and I'm not even a good mother to them. At this point in my story, I'm not only officially a murderer I've also been declared insane by a court and sent here."

He frowned at her as she lit up a stick, drew the smoke into her lungs and blew it into his face.

"You shouldn't be smoking in here Tola, I thought we'd agreed on that."

He stood up, switched off the air-conditioner and threw the windows open. Tola responded by blowing more of the smoke into the air. Morieba's wealth was an insulation, even within the borders of an asylum.

"Now let's picture, for one insane minute, that I got 'better'," she continued as he resumed his seat, "and got discharged from this hospital, what are my chances of making anything of myself in the real world? Where will I live? What will I do with myself Dr Kabir I-know-what-ails-you? Who will employ me, and to do what?" She smoked the cigarette steadily until it burnt to the stub. "No answers sir?"

The doctor made to say something but Tola held up a hand and burst into laughter.

"So what's funny?" He asked, his elbows were on the table, his chin on his palms.

"I just remembered something about laughter and people who've been diagnosed with one form of mental illness or the other." She fiddled with a pen previously lying on the table. "Yoruba people believe that the first sign of madness is excessive laughter. I just realised that I will have to monitor how I laugh. I have to find a balance between not laughing at all and laughing at everything I find amusing… and these days, a lot of things strike me as funny."

"You seem to have forgotten that you're quite a talented artist." Dr. Kabir said quietly.

She ignored his comment, "I don't care much about my parents." Her being talented was not something she wanted to talk about, she did not consider herself particularly talented, she was just venting the darkness inside. "I already told you that my dad died a few years ago. My mum though, she is a character. I'm trying to remember any time in my life that I loved that woman. I must have loved her once. All children do, but right now I can't remember when it was I loved her, that I didn't fear her more than I loved her. She never wanted love from us, she wanted to be feared, she wanted to come back from her teaching job and find us all scrambling about the house putting things straight. There was a time she owned a Peugeot 404 saloon car, she'd start honking loudly as soon as she hit the turning to our street. In case any of us was in a neighbour's house." She shook her head ruefully.

"She enjoyed our fear, the slightest transgression was met with a slap across your face or earned you a beating from her special koboko. From when I turned eight, and until I moved out of our home, she used to whip me every day with a special prayer broom. That wasn't even counted as punishment, it was part of her prayers to keep the demons out of me."

She stood up suddenly and started pacing the office.

"Why don't we sit down more comfortably?" He asked in his I-schooled-in-England voice. Without waiting for an answer he stood up and guided her to a corner of his office which had three couches, done in burgundy.

A shaded lamp stood on one of the two stools placed in-between the chairs. It looked quite homey and intimate.

He sat across from her, crossed his legs and fiddled with the tape recorder he had placed on the dark brown wooden table between them.

He had a disconcerting way of looking at her. The look was cast from the corners of his eyes, sly, a smile playing around his lips.

"Mother is one of those women fond of condemning people. Nobody can do anything right in her sight. She belongs to a particular church where women are not allowed to do a lot of things including wearing any kind of jewellery and certain clothes. When I was growing up my mother didn't allow us to have friends, she was afraid somebody might infect us with demons."

She stretched a leg on the table and looked at him through the corner of her eyes to check for any reaction, his face was immobile. She smiled, placed the other leg on the table and leaned back in satisfaction.

"They used to fight in those days, mother and father, they had big dramatic quarrels at the end of which father usually beat the living daylights out of her. They fought on a regular basis, every fortnight as a matter of course. It was a kind of choreographed dance. They would allow a lot of little annoyances to build up until the tension in the house became quite unbearable and then 'pow!' they would explode. After giving her a beating he would storm out of the house only to return bearing gifts and a remorseful face. Mother would lock him out of her room, he would stay outside their bedroom door beseeching her to forgive him, it was the devil. The devil took over father a lot in those days."

The words flowed, they were unstoppable, this day was a day for words. She had never been this vocal with Dr. Know-it-all medicine. The pills no longer bothered her, she'd stopped swallowing them. She'd learnt how to tuck them into the recesses of her cheeks, spitting them out as soon as the nurses left her room.

"No matter how much he had beaten mother, eventually she would open the door, quoting a Bible passage. One of her standard responses was that 'wives must submit themselves to their husbands as the church submits to God-' or something which allowed her to forgive him for being a beast. Then they would lock bedroom door. It was when I grew older that I realised they were having sex.

It is shocking, you know, the thought that your parents have sex. I mean you'd think that the fact that you are here shows that somebody had sex. The thought that one's parents actually touch each other in an intimate manner can be quite . . ." She paused and looked at him. "When did you realize that your parents have sex?"

"This is not about me Tola, it is all about you." He laughed then put his hand on his chin and gave her a quizzical look.

"Mother did not like a lot of people, because she believed everybody, except her and maybe her favourite pastor, was going to hell. She made sure we know all about hell, its tortures and burning fires. Heaven is too far off and one isn't too sure about the logistics of getting there except one takes extreme measures, for example lopping off parts of one's body when it causes an offence. I actually toyed with the idea of lopping off my mother's tongue. I doubt if it will count as a limb though." She trailed off, the image of blood filling her head.

"For her hell is real." She picked up her narrative. "She had the description down pat and knew all about the sins that can get one there. One look from Mother was all that she needed to know whether you were going to heaven or hell.

"Hell is real, Dr Kabir, and it's not somewhere far off where there are burning fires, and pits filled with poisonous snakes and scorpions. Hell was in my home, it is in my head. I live there. I've lived there since I was eight years old.

"Mother knew about the devil too, the handsome rogue. His wiles, his plan to take over the world in some twisted way. What am I even saying? He has taken over the world already. The only people saving the world from total annihilation are people like mother, the prayer warriors, fanatics, who fear even their shadows — people that call on God at every waking moment.

"I believe there's a devil, his name is Olori Ebi. The only difference between mother's devil and mine is that hers is very good looking, not some overweight Ibadan man who shouts his commands to the four winds, while strutting around like bull in a china shop . . . the quintessential 'African' man with control issues.

"I wonder how mother knew about the sins of the flesh so intimately. The way she delighted in describing those sins intricately, she usually sounded like someone who would have enjoyed sinning. Have I told you that my mother is a pastor? She's a 'deliverance' minister in her church." Tola sneered the word 'deliverance'. She lit up another cigarette. "You should see her using broom to whip the devil out of witches and wizards, she specialized in children deliverance."

She studied the cigarette in-between her fingers. "I remember the day I told my mum that my dad was sexually molesting me, she beat all my demons out of me, all the while speaking in unknown tongues. Beelzebub was the only name I recognized after she had reeled out the names of all the evil spirits in possession of my eight year old body.

"After I had cried myself dry, she then sat me down and called me a slut and said that she'd suspected all along that I'd been having sex. She told me about a certain light in my eyes that did not bode well for my future. The way I defied her and played with other children in the neighbourhood. The way I never rushed around, like a beheaded chicken, anytime she arrived from her office. The way I looked her in the eye when I spoke to her, instead of staring at my feet and shuffling them. I was a changeling with nothing but bad things in my future. She said that God sent me to her to test her faith. It has always been all about her. Turns out she was right about my evil future."

She fell quiet.

"Do you believe all the things she said about you?" Dr. Kabir asked. She ignored the question and continued from where she left off. "She believed I was not meant to go to school, since I always managed to fail all my subjects magnificently and had to repeat some classes. How can the child of a teacher fail? She decided it would be better I was married off at an early age, before I did something that would permanently besmirch the family name. She had never understood me even when I was a baby.

"She then warned me never to repeat the rape story in her presence again and that if she hears of it from anybody else, the beating I had received was a small measure of what she would do to me.

she promised to make marks on my privates and add pepper to it, so that I would never forget. Like I could ever forget her reaction even without the threat. I was just eight years old." she whispered.

Dr. Kabir handed her a handkerchief, she took it without a word and wiped tears off her face.

"I really need to leave."

She stood up abruptly and left the room.

it is with great reluctance that the butterfly enters the bush

Moremi and Morieba pulled to a stop in front of Olori Ebi's house and alighted from the car. While Morieba fetched a bag out of the car, Moremi took a minute to gape at the house which gleamed in the afternoon sunshine with fresh yellow paint. She searched for a word to describe it but came up empty handed.

As they walked towards the gate, she couldn't help comparing it with neighbouring houses, most of which were bungalows with faded paints. The two storied building with all sorts of cement sculptures protruding from it was a peacock amongst a group of peahens.

They opened the gate and walked on interlocked bricks to the front door. She stepped back to look at the building as Morieba rang the bell. When nobody came to the door, Morieba adjusted the folds of her agbada and rang the bell again. After waiting a few more minutes they finally heard approaching footsteps, the door was thrown open by Iyawo, a snotty nosed baby balanced on her hip.

Iyawo smiled, "Anti Morieba, Anti Moremi, good afternoon," she curtsied, "You're welcome," she stepped aside and allowed them into the hallway.

"Good afternoon Iyawo, you're looking well," Morieba said.

"Ah thank you," She hesitated at the bottom of the staircase, "I guess you've come to see your father."

Moremi and Morieba exchanged startled glances.

"Oh yes," Morieba coughed, "can you kindly tell him we're around?"

"So you haven't heard," Iyawo said, "Your father suffered heart attack about two months ago, in fact we just returned from the hospital."

Iyawo's insistence on referring to Olori Ebi as their father grated on Moremi's nerves.

Morieba made sad noises in her throat. "We didn't hear anything Iyawo, maybe it's because we've been out of the country. But you could have dropped a message for us at my house."

Iyawo shifted the baby to her other hip, "Brother Tafa, has been so kind, following us to the hospital and helping out, I thought somebody would have told you."

"I didn't hear anything from anybody, I'm so sorry." Morieba fiddled with the bag. "Does that mean we won't be able to see him?"

"He's lying down in his room. I will go and tell him you're here." Iyawo opened the sitting room door for them.

"It's alright if he can't see us," Morieba sat on the closest chair to the door. "If you just fetch Amope for us, we'll come and see him some other time."

Iyawo froze at the mention of Amope's name. "I will tell Olori Ebi you're here." She almost ran out of the sitting room.

A few minutes later Moremi felt Olori Ebi's presence. He strode into the room like the raw harmattan wind. He did not spare them a glance as he painfully manoeuvred himself onto his favourite chair. After a few minutes of fumbling with his oversized clothes he finally looked at them, his old smile played around his lips.

"Lakiriboto and her apprentice have come out to play," he laughed at his own joke.

"You are a disgusting old man." Morieba fired back unsympathetically. "I thought they said you were knocking at death's door."

lakiriboto chronicles

Olori Ebi bared his teeth at her. "Oh, that's why you're here abi? You think I'm one foot in the grave. But you forget that I'm anikulapo, the one that holds death in his pocket, the one who never dies."

"I know you have the medicine for death Raufu," Morieba smiled mirthlessly, "the same one your father, Saka, and his father, Amuda used. Tell me, did they pass on the medicine to you from their graves?"

"You are a disrespectful woman who will never have children! You think playing mommy to other people's children will give you happiness? I'm so sorry for your sick, depraved and senseless life!" Olori Ebi breathed heavily, his body shook with anger, "Do you think that money can bring you happiness?"

Morieba sucked her teeth, "It is only the dead who can be sure of those who will bury them." She waved a dismissive hand, "and if money can't bring happiness I wonder why you've spent the better part of your life trying to become rich, 'trying' is the operative word here. At least as far as I can see you haven't even built a house of your own," She rolled her eyes. "I'm not here to exchange banter with you and please your twisted ego."

Olori Ebi looked as if he was about to burst, but he pulled a rein on his temper. "So, Madam Lakiriboto what brings your royal highness into our humble house?" As he adjusted himself on the chair, Moremi noted that he listed towards his left side.

"I might be here to throw you out of this house, which now belongs to me." Morieba opened the bag she was carrying and pulled out a folder which she waved in the air.

Olori Ebi straightened in his seat, he growled. "What do you mean by that?"

"Is the great anikulapo going deaf?" Morieba raised her voice, enunciating each word clearly, "this house belongs to me!"

She rifled through the papers in the folder. "So does your office complex, and the family lands in Alagbado. Look here," she smiled and waved another bunch of documents in the air, "the title deeds to Alhaja's properties!"

Moremi watched as the cogwheels of his mind kicked into motion, she knew exactly when he put two and two together and arrived at the correct answer.

His eyes became slits. "You set out to ruin me." He bit out through stiff lips. "You sent those scammers to me."

Morieba shrugged. "Stop whining Olori Ebi and grow up. You started the game, I simply finished it for you!"

"How dare you talk to me like that, you worthless woman?" He yelled.

"I dare do anything I like, because I am a human being just like you. I am not anybody's property whose life can be toyed with. I am not a child who doesn't know her own mind. I am not an idiot to be used and blackmailed by a stupid old man, I am! I am Lakiriboto, that woman who haunts your nightmares!" Morieba was half out of the chair. She punched the air, her middle finger guiding every dagger that flew out of her mouth home.

Olori Ebi grabbed his chest and made mewling tortured cat sounds. Iyawo rushed in at that point, she had a glass of water and some pills in her hands. She glared at the women before giving the pills and water to Olori Ebi. "Please anti Morieba, can't you see he's a sick old man?" She chided them as she fussed over her husband. "And anti Moremi you're just sitting there-"

"Shut up woman!" Olori Ebi threw the half drunk glass of water at Iyawo, missing her head by a few inches. "Get out of here! You are very stupid and presumptuous! Who sought your opinion?"

Moremi felt sorry for the woman as she scurried out of the room.

Olori Ebi rested his back on the chair and shut his eyes. For a few minutes the room went quiet. He eventually opened his eyes, straightened up and looked at the two women.

"What do you want from me?" He asked tiredly.

"Nothing, I have taken everything you've ever had from you, you have nothing I desire." Morieba shrugged off her agbada and flicked the sleeves back on her shoulders, in the classic 'one thousand, five hundred naira' gesture, mastered by all affluent Yoruba women, from birth.

He passed a hand over his brow, "So what are you doing here then?"

"We've come to fetch Amope and then we'll be on our way." Morieba said.

"I don't know what you're talking about." His voice was a brick wall.
"We know she's here, we have proof!" Moremi shouted.
He took his penetrating gaze away from Morieba and focussed on Moremi, he smiled. "It is when a child does not recognize medicine that she calls it spinach. Let me tell you a bedside story child." He addressed his words at Moremi.
"We did not come here to listen to tales by moonlight," Morieba snapped, "You either fetch Amope, or I will find her myself, and man, you won't like it."
"But you will listen to this one, after all, you have cornered a wounded lion, and it will break you in half with its powerful jaws," he said in dulcet tones.
"You really are deluded old man, lion ko, chicken ni!"
Olori Ebi went on with his story, his attitude daring Morieba to fulfil her promise. "There was a boy born into a big family. His father had been married several times to several women over the years. Some of the women still lived with him, while the others had died or divorced him. This innocent child was born by the youngest of the wives, a woman who had been previously engaged to another man."
Moremi shifted in her seat as Olori Ebi's gaze seemed to pierce through her soul.
"She loved this man deeply, he was the one her heart had been bound to since they were toddlers. They had plans, big plans, he was going to send her to school, she would become a nurse, or a teacher, she would become anything she wanted to be, they would love each other till death,"
Moremi knew who the story was about.
"But her dreams were cut short as she was forcefully married to a rich older man by her family because they owed him money. He would forgive their debt and she would provide him the much sought-after male child, who despite marrying many women, had only girls. Two years later, this woman gave the old man a son and while her son was barely three years old she died, she died of a broken heart. As it happens under such circumstances the toddler was given over to be raised by his stepmothers, a bunch of women who were more wicked than witches. The boy was treated like a sub-

human being, although his father loved him, these women ensured that his life was hell on earth. They passed him amongst one another like an unwanted package, sometimes they fed him, sometimes they don't, nobody paid attention to him…"

Moremi was beginning to find the story a tad melodramatic, so she was relieved when Morieba clapped, "Can we do this quickly? You bore me with this your oft repeated story that becomes even more wildly exaggerated at each new telling."

Still ignoring Morieba, Olori Ebi launched into the different ills that were visited on the boy, which included asking him to do household chores, to assist his half-sisters in cooking and fetching water, but he had lost her at the point about wicked stepmothers.

Why are stepmothers always wicked? Is there a handbook that shared amongst them in their secret meetings with titles like 'Wicked Stepmothering 101?'

"That's not all," Olori Ebi was still at it, "when I came into my own, that was when the family came crawling back, they wanted me to come and head them, I was rich enough now to be their son–"

"You're such a liar Olori Ebi, such a big fat liar!" A female voice interrupted his flow.

Moremi looked away from Olori Ebi to the newcomer and her eyes tangled with those of a woman she hadn't seen in over 13years. Her eyes were flat and cold, disinterested.

She snatched her gaze from hers, a mental shrug.

Amope was thin to the point of emaciation, her hair was a shock of grey tight curls on her head. She was wearing a pair of faded jeans and a short sleeved shirt in a shade of dirty brown. Stick like arms that poked out of the shirt was pockmarked with scars, but her face remained the same.

Moremi recoiled; this was the woman who had brought her into the world to be abused by anybody willing to. She'd always thought that women like her mother should be locked up and given forceful abortions anytime they attempted to have children, because the only person they cared about was themselves.

"Why don't you tell them about how spoilt you were?" Amope shut the door behind her and entered the room properly, arms folded

lakiriboto chronicles

across her chest. "Tell them how the other children, except you, were sent to the farm on weekends. How the old man got you your own housemaid and won't allow anybody near you. You were his little prince!"

Shee walked towards them in measured strides.

"Tell them how you stole the little money your stepmothers had. How you dropped out of school and ran away to become a motor-park tout in Ibadan as soon as your father died. Tell them how my mother rescued you from the motor-park and took you in the first time you were accused of armed robbery. Tell them!" Her voice rang out.

Moremi and Morieba jumped out of the seats on which they'd been riveted.

"Tell them how you introduced me to hard drugs while you were living underneath my mother's roof…" Her voice broke.

"Enough of the drama Amope," Morieba said impatiently as she grabbed her bag and Moremi. "We will have enough time to talk about all these things."

"You are not going anywhere! Not with those papers!" With surprising speed Olori Ebi sprung out of his chair and blocked their exit. "You mere children think you can beard the lion in his den and get away unscathed." He drew himself up to his full height and stretched out his hand.

"Give me those papers!" He commanded.

Morieba burst into laughter, "You're joking right? Old man, move out of my way."

Olori Ebi dipped his hand into the folds of his agbada, and pulled out a live tortoise that fitted snugly into his left palm.

Morieba doubled over in hysterical laughter and clapped her hands in derision. "If your jazz is so powerful why hasn't it worked before?"

Olori Ebi stretched the tortoise towards Moremi, Morieba and Amope in short sharp thrusts, thrice, all the while chanting incantations at the top of his lungs.

The ground underneath my feet pay attention to my words, the skies above lend me your ears. It is I, Raufu Motilewa Aguntasoolo, the son of

Arowosegbe who summon you this day. My words take charge of the elements for I hold authority on the palm of my hands.
He stretched out his hand to the four corners of the room.
East, West, North, South, hear the sound of my voice and lend me your ears. For it is what we tell the attentive leaf that it understands. It is what we tell the receptive leaf that it accepts. It is with great reluctance that a butterfly enters the bush.
He used his left hand to fetch a tiny gourd from another pocket, and tapped on the tortoise thrice, threw some of its content on its shell and touched it with the tip of his tongue thrice. The tortoise poked its head out of its shell slowly.
Moremi, just like her mother and aunt were frozen to the spot, the only thing she could process was how much the scene fascinated and repulsed her. The room was heavy with an otherworldly presence as Olori-Ebi appeared to grow bigger, bigger than her sane mind knew he could ever be. He filled the room, his head nearly touching the ceiling, the tortoise cradled in his palm seemed to be grinning.
Somebody was calling her name, but the voice was coming from afar. Olori Ebi was the only real thing, he filled her eyes, her senses, everything else was background noise. She stared at the tortoise, it drew her into itself, into the slow churning of its thoughts. Nothing else existed but Olori Ebi's tortoise, his voice.
It can never be well with a never-do-well. Things never work out for taboo breakers The pestle can never find a place of rest...
Moremi snapped out of the spell as Olori Ebi fell to the ground with a thud. Standing by the door, with a bewildered look on his face, was Quadri.
"What's going on here?" He asked as Morieba knelt beside Olori Ebi's supine form, and fetched her phone out of her pocket.
"Hello, ambulance services? It's an emergency, yes I know it's a private service, I'm a client! Come to No. 3, Idi-Ikan."

deliverance

Tola was standing in front of her easel, painting the man of her dreams. The man was black, a solid brick wall of darkness, he was tall, he was headless, an emptiness stood in place of his penis. His arms were outstretched, powerful, well-defined arms, nailed to an invisible cross.

Tola dipped her brush in the paint and slashed a trail of red down his torso. Her eyes were inside, seeing the line of blood trailing from its neck down to the empty spot between his spread-eagled legs.

The vision disappeared as the click-click of uneven heels reached her hearing. She expelled an angry breath, knowing without a doubt that she wouldn't be able to do anything further until the footsteps stopped. They didn't, only drew closer and closer to her workspace.

"They've arrived." she muttered.

Through the corners of her eyes, she noted that the other inmates that were with her in the studio were dropping their tools and clearing out their workspaces. Clenching her jaws, Tola tightened her grip on the brush and focussed on the canvas. Her hand froze as the footsteps stopped beside her, she curled her toes and groaned.

"Good afternoon Miss Tola."

His deep voice set her teeth on edge.

"What do you want?" She dropped her paintbrush. She did not look at him.

"Remember I told you the Senior Pastor promised to come today?" His voice was full of cheer.

Tola squeezed her eyes shut and drew in a breath, ruing again, the day she had smiled back at him.

His name was Chizoba, he was a fine specimen of man. All white teeth, yellow skin and muscles that showed through his shirt. He reminded her of the men that had visited Rita in the darkened rooms of Isale-Eko. He smelled like them, earthy, sweaty, pheromones clogging up the air.

He came to the asylum, regularly, with a bunch of other do-good-two-shoes that came to preach, or as he put it 'fellowship', with the inmates. She had kept clear of them for a whole year, mainly because of the women.

While the men dressed in trousers, with well ironed shirts tucked neatly into the waistband, thick leather belts adding a touch of style, the women dressed in the long gowns and skirts discarded by Victorians on their way out of Nigeria. Their scarves were bound tightly around their head, creating deep furrows between their foreheads and eyebrows.

The women reminded her of her mother. They looked at you with a promise of the hell that awaited you, after the one you'd been through on earth. They had the fire of fanaticism burning bright in their yellowed gazes. They looked like they'd never experienced an orgasm before in their lives.

Sometimes, when she watched them from behind her bedroom curtains, she would be tempted to spread her good news to them... about how they should consider spreading their legs and discover that heaven was not as far from them as they imagined.

But a few months earlier, during one afternoon of weakness, when she had been at her most needy of human contact, humans who were not inmates of the asylum in the guise of doctors, or nurses, or patients, Chizoba had walked up to her on the corridor with pearly whites, and she had smiled back.

He had not left her alone since then.

He'd talk to her whether she responded or not. He would knock on her bedroom door, stalk her on the corridors, follow her into the studio. Whenever she bothered to pay him some attention, he would smile into her eyes and tell her the 'good news of Jesus Christ' and the bad news of the horrid world outside the asylum gates.

He told her about a heaven whose streets were paved with gold, where everything she had always wanted would be handed to her on a platter, just because.

Whenever she was in a teasing mood and she pointed out that there were also rumours about the streets of New York being paved with gold, he would go into a long, earnest, discourse about faith being the hope of what was not seen.

She liked the way he would squint his eyes, his body poised as if he

wanted to shove 'faith' into her head.
In this heaven of his 'there shall be no sadness', even the lion and the lamb lay peacefully side by side.

Maybe they prefer gazelle cuttings.

He painted her the picture of muscular, Aryan angels with peace as wings, who were waiting to serenade her with their cherubic songs for all eternity - in this white heaven. A heaven so white she told him nobody would let her in, on account of her dark soul, and more so, because of her dark skin.

But he said it was alright, although none of the angels had black skin and the god, the one and only true god, he called him, the all-white god with his huge... white beard, would welcome her home with a hug.

He told her all she needed was to confess Jesus Christ as her lord and saviour, and her dark soul would become as white as snow.

Since only souls go to heaven that means I'll be white too, so it's alright.

"Shall we proceed to the fellowship now?" Chizoba asked.

Tola frowned and looked at him for the first time. "I asked what you want from me."

The coldness in her tone must have finally pierced his thick skin because he took a step back and cleared his throat. "You promised to attend the service if our Senior Pastor comes visiting."

She took a step towards him. "I told you that I don't like church." He backed off, she followed him. "I never got any help when I was in the church, all I got was pressurised to become the neck, a submittee, mother, friend, wife, holy ... everything I was not. They wanted to turn me into something not totally human!"

Heavy footsteps stopped their dance.

"Is there any problem Brother Chizoba?"

Tola's head whipped towards Nurse Lim, a giant of a man with deep tribal marks scored from the tips of his lips to his cheeks.

"No there isn't." Tola stepped away from Chizoba.

"Like, like, she said," Chizoba stuttered. "There isn't, only the Senior Pastor would like to meet with our new converts and I thought Miss

Tola would like that." He finished on a rush.

She sucked her teeth, "What part of I-do-not-like don't you understand?"

Tola had discarded her pretend-shyness along with her meds and weaves. She had embraced her madness, found her voice. She would no longer be silenced.

A heavy hand descended on her shoulder.

"You should calm down Tola, nobody is forcing you to do anything against your will." Nurse Lim was being reasonable. His hand bit into her shoulder. "It's just that everybody else has left for the service and I won't want to leave you by yourself in the studio."

Tola's shoulders slumped as the futility of arguing with them hit her.

In the early days she'd spent so many hours strapped down to a table, drugged to her eyeballs. She didn't want a repetition of that, so she relaxed and flashed them a smile.

"I didn't know that, you mean everybody is in the cafeteria?" she asked just to be sure.

"Yes, everybody, even the Chief Medical Officer." Chizoba boasted. "My senior pastor is a very powerful man. The power of god is always with him, he might even deliver you–"

"Deliver me from what?" She stopped in her tracks and faced him squarely, fists clenched.

"Relax Tola," Nurse Lim was there, standing next to her, his bulk placed in a manner that needed no words. Her fists unclenched of their own accord.

"I'm sure you'll enjoy the service." He smiled down at her. "I heard they have really nice music and there'll be cake."

She smiled faintly, being in an asylum means you're stupid, unpredictable, someone to be offered cake as Èsù would be offered palm oil.

She nodded and moved away from the two men, "Let's go there."

"Thank you so much Nurse Lim." Chizoba shouted cheerily as he ran after her.

The cafeteria was packed by the time they got there. Aside from the inmates, who were seated duly, on white plastic chairs, there were also doctors and nurses, nursing attendants and even some guards that manned the gates. Tola stood firmly at the back, resisting Chizoba's suggestion that they move forward.

Chizoba stood possessively by her side, she was his soul, he had won her.

Nurse Lim slid in and found an empty seat in the centre of the room. Tola enjoyed how he stepped on people's toes to get to the seat.

The microphone spit static drawing her gaze to the podium, where a jerry-curled, light skinned man stood. He was sweating profusely underneath the three piece suit he had on, a microphone was clutched to his chest. Three hefty men in dark sunglasses stood guard around the podium. The pastor's head bounced up and down as he preached in an unintelligible language to the enraptured audience who, once in a while, would shout an 'Amen' or 'Alleluyah' to whatever it was he had been saying.

"Batsesheba! Rumunumu! Rumpelstiltskin!" The man shouted into the microphone... at least that was what Tola heard, eyes filled with amusement met the pastor's. She registered with faint surprise that she'd seen him on television before.

"You!" He pointed at her.

Tola looked over her shoulder just to be clear.

"Bring that young lady over here! Tha Lor' tol' me tudaay, is your day of freedom!"

The congregation erupted into shouts of 'halleluyah' and 'amen' as she was half pushed, half pulled down the aisle, by the ushers who had run to her side immediately the pastor pointed at her.

She was thrust forward suddenly, and found herself in front of the podium. The pastor raised his voice higher, a feat she would never have thought possible, "Bobirigiri, ripompolisti, orangey, limpopo, zambezi!" He pointed heavenwards, Tola looked up, expecting a rain of gold.

"Loose her, in Jesus name!" He jumped down from the podium and struck her on the forehead.

Tola blanked out, Rita grabbed the pastor's arm, flipped him over her head and heard a satisfying snap, as she knelt sharply on his wrist.

"I am god!" She whispered fiercely. Ran for the wide window closest

to the podium and jumped through it, she didn't look back.
Rita ran.
She ran past her hostel block, past some doctors and nurses who ignored her, used to seeing her running around. She ran past some inmates that were probably headed for the cafeteria. She ran steadily, she did not make eye contact with anybody.
She ran until she got to the abandoned building where she'd hidden the things she might need when the time was and it had come. She pulled off her grey uniform, wore the knee length knickers, boots, a long curly wig, sunshades and a face-cap.
She stepped into an inner room of the uncompleted building and pulled up the stone that had been her bank for nearly eight months. She didn't pause to check how much she had been able to save, she placed the bundle of money in her pocket.
It had taken her eight months to salt away all the things she would need for her escape. Eight months of patience and cunning. Her time was up. The guards and nurses were searching for her by now, she didn't want to think about the police.
She took off in a rapid walk, she couldn't run for fear of attracting attention. Within five minutes she was at the far end of the hospital compound, heading for the break in the wall that she had explored several times. Behind the wall was a huge maize farm. She plunged into it, maize leaves and stalks scratched her bare arms and legs, but she didn't pause, her legs squashed maize stalks, arms waved wildly before her face.
After about thirty minutes of trotting as fast as she dared through several farms, she finally broke through to a tiny footpath and followed it.
In the months following the day her escape plans had been outlined for her by Èsù, Rita had spent more and more time exploring the asylum grounds, following the directions she'd written down immediately she came out of her trance, well not trance, more like hallucination.
Èsù had appeared to her as a woman/man. S/he had been indescribably beautiful, not that Rita could even if she tried. S/he had loosened the straps binding Rita to the table, helped her to sit up

and offered her a sip of vodka, heavenly vodka. After a while they had handed her a pen and paper and had given her, in great details, how she would escape from the asylum. Rita had asked when she should leave, they had smiled and told her to be patient.

If Tola hadn't woken up clutching that piece of paper and a little lightheaded from the copious amounts of vodka and chocolate Èsù had shared with her, she would have dismissed the experience as another phase of her mental illness.

As soon as she'd been let out of solitary confinement, she had started taking regular walks around the hospital, particularly in the directions she'd written down on the paper. Her explorations had only taken her to the uncompleted building, the break in the wall and a little way into the maize farm.

The footpath confirmed that she was right trusting Èsù, because she knew there was a small village nearby, and freedom.

She fished out the rumpled sheet of paper, which contained her plans and Morieba's phone numbers. She'd been told Morieba would hide her. She smiled happily and returned the paper to her pocket as she spotted the village. From her vantage point on top of a small hill, she noted that there weren't more than 20 houses in the village, it wasn't a village, a hamlet.

She half slid, half ran down the hill and spotted a wider path that seemed to run through the centre of the hamlet. Feeling energized, she trotted towards it.

She was soon surrounded by naked children who stared at her open mouthed. Silent parents came and dragged their children away.

"Good afternoon madam." Rita called out to a woman seated in front of her hut, eating rice out of a pot burnt black by woodsmoke. "Please ma, I'm going to Abeokuta, can you show me the way?"

The woman took in Rita's shorts and shirt with one sweeping glance. "Good afternoon." She pointed down the sandy road, "Keep walking in that direction," She pointed down the path, "you will get to the expressway, but it's very far. Do you want me to call my son to take you there on his bike?"

Taken by surprise at the woman's kindness, Rita replied shyly that she wouldn't mind.

"But you will have to buy fuel for him."
The woman rose from her seat and offered Tola the stool. She entered the house and returned some minutes later.
"He's gone to fetch the bike, he'll soon be here."
True to her words a few minutes later a Jingcheng bicycle roared to a stop in front of the hut.
Tola climbed aboard, thanking the woman profusely.
The silent young man drove her to the expressway. "Wait here madam, cars going to Abeokuta pass through here."
"Where does the road on the other side lead to?" Tola asked out of curiousity.
"Ibadan."
"Oh good, so if I cross to the other side I will find buses going to Ibadan."
"Yes ma."
Tola smiled at him as she alighted from the bike and gave him almost half of the bunch of money in her pocket. The young man smiled in delight as he accepted the money. He thanked her and offered to help her cross the expressway.
"I'll be alright, thank you so much."
Tola waved at him and crossed to the other side. Within five minutes a car pulled up and a young man wearing a sleeveless shirt stuck his head through the window.
"Can I give you a ride?"
The man smelt of sweat, pheromones and dark rooms, Rita flashed him her prettiest smile, and climbed in beside him.
I don't think I'll go to Morieba's just yet...